LOSS OF INNOC

LOSS OF INNOCENCE

A Family's Journey with Meth

Ronald B. Clem
and
Carren LeAnn Clem

Published in Great Britain in 2007 by
Virgin Books Ltd
Thames Wharf Studios
Rainville Road
London
W6 9HA

A catalogue record for this book is available from
the British Library.

The paper used in this book is a natural, recyclable product
made from wood grown in sustainable forests. The
manufacturing process conforms to the regulations of the
country of origin.

ISBN 978 07535 11596 (UK)
ISBN 978 182227 3569 (USA)

Typeset by TW Typesetting, Plymouth, Devon
Printed and bound in Great Britain by
Mackays of Chatham PLC

Child Lost

Face down; the frozen earth her only companion.
A precious life ebbs away; a final breath, another child lost.
Overwhelming pain and anguish, her parents can only wonder why.
For them all that will remain is emptiness, a fading memory, and regret.
As we hold each other, tears and love are all we can share.
Her mother cries, 'I just didn't understand.
She could not fight this battle alone.'
Meth has taken another child.

Ron Clem

DEDICATION

There are many parents we have met over the past five years who have suffered immeasurable pain due to their children's choice to use drugs or create friendships with those participating in the drug culture. Many of these parents no longer have the blessing of their children's presence in their lives. Illicit drug use and the associated violence and suicide resulted in the death of their children. The only thing left for these families are the memories of days past and the hopes and dreams they had for their children's future.

This book is dedicated to all those families and especially to:

Steve and Susan Stapley
Gerri Gardner
Connie Guzman
Greg and Mary Haydal
Dan and Linda Smith
and the Jorgenson Family

The courage they displayed over the loss of their children gave me the courage to go on. Every time I am blessed with the opportunity to hug my daughter I think of each of you. Thank you and may God bless you.

Ron Clem and Carren Clem

CONTENTS

LIST OF ILLUSTRATIONS

Carren, Alicia and Scott living life to its fullest, a true picture of innocence, in the 'Last Best Place.'

We were blessed with three beautiful children, a great marriage, and lived in paradise. Ron, Karyl, Alicia, Carren and Scott.

I loved holding the violin in my hands. It was so delicate and I felt a sense of pride and accomplishment when playing.

Eighth grade confirmation ceremonies administered by Pastor Darold Reiner. Carren stood tall, declaring her Christian values and beliefs.

Carren at age three: I had a great life growing up. I knew my mom and dad loved me and just as important they loved each other.

Carren posing with her mighty steed 'Mickey.' He terrorized Carren's older sister by biting, but was humbled by a mighty blow from Carren's hands.

Carren enjoying life before heading off to the big kids' school in the fall.

SUWS graduation: After 21 days in the Idaho wilderness, the girls and staff hike out for a reunion with family. Mom telling Carren she loves her even though she is a little smelly.

Carren and Karyl posing in the courtyard at the Caribbean Center for change. It was our first official visit and we all agreed: 'There is life after Meth.'

Typical girl's laundry day at TB. Karyl verifying everything is clean and asking, 'You did these all by hand?'

Family Reunion at Tranquility Bay. As the program puts it, 'Making a whole and healthy family.'

Scott's graduation from Marine Boot Camp at the Marine Corps
Recruit Depot, San Diego. A family in healing.

5 years of sobriety, life at its best in the 'Last Best Place',
Yellowstone National Park, Montana and Wyoming.

ACKNOWLEDGEMENTS

The efforts put forth by an author are in part minuscule in comparison with the support and assistance of family, friends, and those asked to provide technical assistance. This was most definitely true for Carren and me when putting our pen to paper. We wish to thank first and foremost our family for loving us and supporting our efforts, especially Karyl, mother and wife, the consummate giver; Alicia Clem, for loving us in spite of our faults, and Scott Clem, Corporal, US Marine Corps; Semper Fi son: Thank each of you for your love and patience.

To the many friends that took the time to review our original writings: Mike McGrath, Montana State Attorney General, Robert Dupont, MD, author and treatment specialist, Alex Stalcup, MD, treatment specialist, Lynn and Colleen St Pierre, Gary and Kim Anderson, Linda and Dan Smith, Norm and Glenda Davis, John and Deanna Hale, Greg and Mary Haydal, Marty and Pam Pomeroy, Paul Jacobs, Tom Allen, Rex and Susan Boller, John and Karen Weaver, and Cindy Branch, Editor of *Montana Woman Magazine*. And finally, a special thank you to all those that are fighting the good fight, on a daily basis, to save our children: child protective services, health and human services, local police and sheriffs' agencies, community outreach programs, emergency fire and hospital personnel, and those special teachers and counselors that have dedicated their lives to our children. Thank each and every one of you.

Thank you and God's blessings.

Carren LeAnn Clem and Ronald B. Clem

DISCLAIMER

Due to the nature of the topics and events portrayed in the account of our family's lives, it has been necessary to alter many names, places, and events to protect other innocent individuals or their families. All accounts relating to our family's experience are true – although to be honest I wish many were not.

1. THE PREAMBLE TO PARENTING

*The worst horror a mom or dad can experience is the death of their child.
It's impossible to comprehend the pain and horrible sense of loss, the
forever emptiness. Maybe that's why so many of us pull away from
grieving parents: we just don't know what to do or say. The thought it
could happen to one of our children is too unbearable. Yet when I think
back, I often welcomed death for my little girl and at times I actually
prayed for it; I just couldn't stand the thought of her going through
another minute, another day, pursuing her only love in life – meth.*

Ron Clem

Never in my wildest dreams did I plan on being called Daddy
by my three children. My father left home when I was six or
seven years old and Mom was left with the responsibility of raising
my sister and me. She worked nights as a waitress, yet there never
seemed to be enough money to make ends meet.

Being young at the time, I didn't understand all that was going
on, but within a few months of Dad's leaving, one of the so-called
proper women caught me taking an extra cookie from the welcome
table after the Sunday morning service. She grabbed me by the back
of my shirt, crushed the cookie in my hand and told me, 'You know
the rules, one cookie only.' As she was walking away she

commented to one of her other decent ladies, 'Those little Clem bastards don't even belong here anyway.' I didn't know what a bastard was. But knew if this lady was saying it, it couldn't be good. In the early Fifties being a divorced family was frowned upon and soon we were shamed into leaving our church. Church life had been the primary focus of my dad's life, and thus had become ours. And now we were without Dad and our church family.

Several months after Dad left, Mom started nursing college and any hope my sister and I had of ever having our mom home again vanished. We always were short of money, which meant food on the table. Mom was a 'good looker' and utilized her talents in dating to feed us kids. More often than not, if some guy wanted to take Mom out it required feeding us kids first. Eventually we qualified for welfare, but until that time Mom did whatever was necessary to survive. At times my sister and I heard some of the adults in the neighborhood use words like 'whore' when talking about Mom, but it was always in a hush and we weren't supposed to hear.

The only real family I remember was Morris's, my best friend: his mom and dad would feed me occasionally and didn't mind dolling out a little discipline when needed. I started running the streets when I was eight or nine. Early on we formed our own little Rollingwood gang to protect ourselves from the black kids from Parchester Village. When we would walk to school, older blacks – drop outs and the like – would wait for us, beat the crap out of us and take our lunch money. More often than not they terrorized us just for fun.

Our little group never got into any real trouble, mostly annoying pranks and petty vandalism. I must have been about twelve when I had my first encounter with the police. One of our favorite pastimes was 'the blackout raid' this involved shutting off the master electrical power on a 30 unit apartment complex near the main highway. We would listen to the tenants' disgruntled complaints and then take off running. The managers and residents must have gotten pretty tired of our repeated forays, but we always thought if it really bothered them they would put a lock on the panel or something.

One night we made our typical 'blackout raid' and took off running. Before we knew it 15 to 20 residents were chasing us, as well as several police cars. We couldn't believe it; we were just shutting off the lights for crying out loud. The police finally caught us and started shaking us down pretty good. One cop finally revealed why there had been such an intense effort to stop our little prank. It seems that one of the residents in the apartment was suffering from the after effects of polio. He required an iron lung (a cylinder to assist his breathing) and, as it turned out, we almost killed him twice. The police took us down to the station after roughing us up again and then called our parents.

Mom must have told them she was a single mom and could use some help with me. This resulted in another series of shakedowns and threats from the arresting officers. After I had sat in a cell for about four hours Mom showed up to take me home. I was ready: I just knew those officers would have killed me if they kept me any longer.

I attended Richmond High School, in beautiful downtown Richmond, California. This was the high school made famous by the recent movie *Coach Carter*. It was a tough school, packed with way too many kids, overwhelmed by racial tension, and all too often days were highlighted by violence. I did OK in school: I was enrolled in college prep courses and all that kind of stuff, but boredom and too many John Wayne movies finally took its toll. I dropped out of school in my senior year and joined the US Navy. I went to boot camp the day after my seventeenth birthday and ended up celebrating my next birthday in Viet Nam.

Before leaving on my first tour to Viet Nam, I was granted a much-needed seven-day pass. I headed home, arriving at Mom's in time for a high-school friend's wedding the next day. Mike was a year older than me and had joined the Navy a little over a year earlier. He had just returned from his first tour to Viet Nam that week. His wedding on Saturday was to be a big event and everyone was planning on celebrating his transition into bondage. Mike's mom lived in the same apartment complex with Mom and as soon as I got home we made plans for his bachelor's party that evening. I needed transportation and decided to take my motorcycle out of storage. It needed a little cleaning and tender loving care, and while washing it off outside, Mike came over and asked if he could take my motorcycle for a ride. I hadn't even ridden it myself yet, but what the heck – it was his last day of freedom. Mike zoomed out of the parking lot, a big smile on his face, yelling as he looked back at me, 'I shall return.'

I walked up the stairs to put away the cleaning gear and Mom asked where Mike was going. Just for a ride around the block, I replied. Mike said it was his last chance of freedom before the big day and we both laughed. His soon to be wife forbade him from riding motorcycles, said they were too dangerous. I taunted Mike by asking, 'What does she know?' Ten to fifteen minutes passed and Mike hadn't returned. I was getting a little upset: I had to run a few errands before our party that night. I walked outside to see if he might have returned and I just missed him. Mike's mom called a few minutes later and asked if I knew where Mike was and I replied riding my motorcycle. She said his fiancée was coming over soon; they had an appointment at the church and he had better get back quick.

After an hour I became concerned and started calling the fire departments and police stations. When I told the police why I had called, I was immediately transferred to the patrol sergeant. He asked me for some information about Mike: What was he wearing, his age, and general description. He then asked for the make and license plate number of my motorcycle. As soon I told him the license number, he asked if I could come to the police station. I borrowed Mom's car keys and told her I needed to go to the police station. There had just been an accident between a truck and a motorcycle near my mom's house; they wanted to see if I could identify the driver of the motorcycle.

Mike died instantly in the head on collision with the semi truck. I identified my motorcycle and Mike. Rather than have the police call Mike's mom, I decided to go and tell her in person. I stopped by my house and told Mom what had happened and she came with me to break the horrible news.

Mike's fiancée never forgave me, and to be honest I have never really forgiven myself. I left home early to return back to base and left for Viet Nam a few days later. I had lost a friend and learned a valuable lesson: Life was a precious gift and it can be taken away in an instant.

I met my wife-to-be, Karyl, in southern California during a short stint living with Dad. She was the most beautiful girl I had ever met and although I had no plans on marrying anyone soon, I knew she was the person I was going to live with for the rest of my life. We became engaged just before I left for my second tour of Viet Nam. I wanted my proposal to Karyl to be romantic and, with that in mind, I proposed by playing Jim Reeves's top single hit 'Distant Drums' on the record player. I handed Karyl a stuffed dog with an engagement ring tied around its neck. Karyl started crying and I couldn't figure it out. My sister later told me, 'You dummy, that song is about a young man going off to war. He wanted to get married and in the event he was killed!' What was I thinking?

As I look back to those times, I can't fathom what we were thinking. We were both very young; Karyl was seventeen and I was nineteen years of age. I was a high school dropout and heading back to Viet Nam. After Karyl accepted my proposal, we drove over to tell her mother. Karyl's mom was recently divorced and Karyl knew her mom wasn't going to take the news well. We walked in the door and her mom sensed something was up. We told her we had something important to tell her and wanted her to sit down. I stood proudly and told her I wanted to marry her daughter. I explained to her excitedly that I had proposed to her only daughter, actually her only child, just a few minutes before and Karyl had accepted. Her mom looked up at us, tears filled her eyes and she jumped up and ran from the room crying.

I hadn't quite expected that kind of response. Karyl and I both just stood there staring at each other. After several minutes, actually it seemed like hours, listening to Karyl's mom crying in the next room, Karyl suggested I leave and she would take care of her mom. We weren't planning on getting married until I returned from Viet Nam, which would be in a year's time and Karyl was convinced she could win her mom over by then. The year I spent overseas I received constant letters from Karyl's family, friends, and acquaintances suggesting we wait to get married until I finished high school, had a job, and could adequately provide for her. We were told over and over that we were too young and our marriage would never last, but we were young and in love and unwilling to be dissuaded. Karyl continued to plan the wedding as we both anticipated starting a new life together as soon as I returned.

Karyl and I did marry four days after I returned from Viet Nam. It has been 37 years and she is and has been my best friend and lover ever since. Fortunately for me she was a hard worker as well and willing to support me in my educational endeavors. After my discharge from the Navy, I attended night school at Fullerton Community College and received my high school diploma. Immediately after being honorably discharged from the Navy I pursued a course of study in Biology and received my BS degree from Cal State University, Fullerton in 1973. We never planned to have a family; kids just didn't seem to fit into our – or maybe I should say my – plans.

We were both from divorced families and were constantly haunted by the experiences of our parents' failed marriages. I felt I had something to prove to myself and to Karyl's family: I wasn't just your typical kid from a poor family whose mom had been called a whore for trying to take care of us when we were young. I wasn't stupid just because I was a high school dropout; I wanted to prove I was worthy of being Karyl's husband. Karyl was an only child and had fears of having and raising children as well. We were both committed to being financially successful before having children and to the principle of not allowing our children to experience a broken home. As it turned out, we ended up waiting twelve years before having children and in retrospect that may have been too soon.

After securing my bachelors degree in 1973, I was accepted into a Masters program for Microbiology and was living the not so exciting life of a grad student. I really wasn't enjoying the effort and fortunately happened upon a job fair on campus attended by officers from the Los Angeles Police Department (LAPD), before I knew it I found myself working as a cop in Los Angeles, California.

Being a cop in the early Seventies and Eighties was the experience of a lifetime. There were more urban terror groups running amok than at any time in our history: the Black Liberation Army (BLA), People's Liberation Party (PLP), Symbionese Liberation Army (SLA), Black Panthers, and many others were all active at this time. My first division was Newton Street, located in south-central Los Angeles.

Radio calls came fast and furious and I can remember one of the first: '13A43, 13A43 Officer needs help, shooting in progress, 54th and Compton, shots still being fired, 13A43 handle the call Code 3.' Little did I know, as we roared down the street in our 1967 turbo-charged Plymouth, red lights flashing, siren screaming, and shotguns at the ready, that I would be participating in one of the historic shootouts of the century.

The SLA, led by the infamous Cinque, known for their bank robberies, police car bombings, and the kidnapping of heiress Patricia Hearst, were now barricaded in a shabby, one-story house on the south side of 54th Street. The urban terrorists were armed with automatic weapons, shotguns and numerous handguns. It was a fierce firefight and only ended when fire erupted inside the structure and all the occupants, the self-proclaimed liberators of the oppressed, chose to die in the intense fire, rather than surrender. I guess I never thought that it might have been easier to surrender if they hadn't been shot at every time they stuck their heads out the doors or windows.

One of my first partners was the legendary, and on occasion notorious, Barry Levin. He was known as one of the best narcotics officers working the streets of Los Angeles. Barry was a golden gloves pugilist and, more often than not, could terminate a street fight with a single blow delivered at lightning speed. Barry was my training officer and after mentoring me through hundreds of arrests and never-ending court appearances, I was recognized as a narcotics expert by the courts for identification, under the influence, packaging for sales, and sales of: heroin, cocaine, marijuana, hashish, LSD, and PCP.

Being a drug cop was the highlight of my days working the streets and I never thought for one minute illicit drugs would eventually tear my family apart. After working several other high-intensity geographic areas, Central and Hollenbeck Divisions, I finally made the grade as a tough, hardened, street cop. I never considered that what served me well in surviving the streets in Los Angeles would be my downfall as a dad in later years. I seemed to have lost my sense of compassion and the ability to love or care for anything or anyone.

Working Central Division was an experience of a lifetime, or should I say many lifetimes. Central Division was located in the downtown section of the city and housed most of the indigents, excons, and winos blessing the City of Angels. Fifth Street between Los Angeles Street and Alameda was known as the shit-hole hotel section. Most of the excons that claimed Los Angeles as their home-away-from-home lived in the hundred or so dilapidated hotels, motels and boarding houses stacked side by side, street after street. Los Angeles Street was the center of the low-life gay district containing prostitutes, porno theaters, and sex shops. If you weren't breaking up fights between jealous drag queens, you were peeling drunks off sidewalks for their weekly checkup at the city jail.

I remember the first night we received the call for 'theater check' at one of the porno theaters.

'What is a theater check?' I asked my partner.

'Come with me, boy, and you will soon be enlightened,' he replied.

As we entered one of the many porno theaters, it was obvious they had a premier smut movie in progress. Although visibility was limited due to the dim lighting, you could tell the place was packed. We started walking down the aisles and I could hear empty popcorn bags rattling. My partner took out his nightstick and reached out and whacked one of the bags sitting on a guy's lap. The guy moaned briefly and we moved on. I soon realized that most of the perverts had the popcorn bags over their manhood and were masturbating while watching the movie. I immediately thought, 'God, what am I doing here?'

My partner explained it was our job to encourage each of the over-zealous bag rattlers to wait until they left the theatre for their love experience. One night of patrol in this cesspool left you trying to disinfect everything you wore. More often than not it would have been better to just burn your uniform, because you never got rid of the smell of putrifying urine, ejaculation, feces, or weeks of built-up body odor. The thought that never seemed to leave you after working the downtown ghetto streets of Los Angeles was the overwhelming sense of hopelessness due to the perversion, deca-dence, and lack of value for human life.

I had performed well as a new officer in Central Division and was rewarded by being offered the opportunity to work a plain-clothes Special Problems Unit (SPU). I was working one of the last days of uniformed patrol: My partner and I had just finished our routine check of the shit-hole district and were heading to Code 7 – dinnertime in police talk.

It was just after 8:00 pm and we were heading to the upscale district for a little peace and relaxation. We turned south on Hill Street from 7th and observed a large gathering of Mexican Americans actively kicking and beating a black cab driver who was lying on the ground. He appeared to be severely injured due to the continuous beating by his assailants. From the earnest efforts of his attackers it was obvious the cabbie didn't have long to live if we didn't intercede. I was passenger officer and bailed out of the car just after requesting 'Officer needs assistance, major 415 7th and Hill Streets.'

At first my partner and I thought it was a dispute due to a traffic accident and the altercation started when the parties attempted to establish who was to blame. As I approached the group who were hitting and kicking the cabbie, I couldn't believe what I saw. The assailants were way overdressed for a street fight: There was a young woman dressed in a wedding dress and several young men in suits. I called out, telling them to back off, obviously misjudging the intentions of the now obvious wedding party.

Just as I got close to the group one of the male Latins hit me in the face, knocking me down. Before I knew it they had surrounded me and started kicking me in the head, face, torso and anywhere else their shoes could reach. I yelled for my partner to get help and fought off the blows as best I could. I felt someone trying to pull my revolver from my holster and thought, 'These assholes want to kill me.'

I looked over and saw one of the suspects hit my partner in the face with a whiskey bottle. Blood exploded from his face and he went down. Suddenly I felt a crushing blow on my head and I started to lose consciousness. There must have been at least ten or twelve members of the wedding party taking turns kicking and hitting me and, for the first time since working the streets, I felt I might not make it through this attack.

I was drifting in and out of consciousness and was amazed at not feeling any pain from the repeated blows. Thoughts briefly came to me: Would my wife miss me and what would I look like after they finished kicking my face in? It was a surreal feeling, yet I didn't have an ounce of fear or regret. I kept hearing this distant crushing sound and thought it must be my attackers kicking me in the head. Over and over again this sound kept repeating.

Suddenly I opened my eyes and there was this guy standing over me beating off members of the Mexican wedding party with his ghetto blaster. I could hear the roar of police cars and sirens coming closer and knew help was on the way. I couldn't move and realized if help didn't get here soon my sole rescuer, my knight in shining armor, would not be able to continue beating off my attackers with his rapidly disintegrating prize sound system.

Help finally arrived; my partner and I were transported to the hospital. The Mexican Wedding Party went to jail, and my rescuer eventually received a city award for saving one of the City of LA's finest. I got to visit with the guy who saved my life a few weeks later. He was an ex-con who'd just got out of jail for armed robbery and was currently on parole.

'It just didn't seem right all those bangers beating you like they were,' he said. 'When the police arrested me, they treated me like a man. Those wedding guys weren't treating you like a man, so I thought I would just help out.'

'I'm damn glad you did, James,' I replied and thanked him for helping me. I never saw him again. My injuries at the time didn't seem significant: The most obvious were multiple contusions, abrasions, but I had also sustained a concussion. After several weeks the pain in my stomach and chest area failed to subside and after several tests my doctor and other specialists determined I had a ruptured diaphragm and groin rupture. Over the course of two years I had to be hospitalized four times and ended up having surgery to repair the ruptures and severe stomach and esophageal ulcers.

I eventually transferred out of Central Division and after a brief stint in an administrative unit transferred to Hollenbeck Division in 1982. Hollenbeck was located east of Los Angeles and was predominantly populated by Mexican Americans and illegal Mexican aliens. It was a welcome change from the decadence of Central Division. The majority of the residents in Hollenbeck were families; religious in nature, and for the most part law-abiding citizens. On the flip side there were the Mexican gangs that terrorized the local community, constantly reasserting their control of their turf through murder, assaults, and intimidation. The Mexican gangs – Whitefence, El Sereno, La Familia, Pico Aliso – generated their names based on their specific geographical location where they lived and typically financed their existence through extortion, drug dealing, burglaries and thefts.

It was our job to destabilize whatever gang lived in our patrol area and provide protection for the decent families of East Los Angeles. I loved my job in Hollenbeck and developed strong ties with local residents. I learned to admire their tenacious efforts to support their families and communities. To my partner's and my credit we also became the worst enemy of the local El Sereno Gang. We felt it our duty to make their criminal activity a constant invitation to the city and county jails. Granted they often didn't spend a lengthy time behind bars but we were content to provide them a life sentence via the installment plan.

Our efforts worked and we were rewarded with Officer of the Year by the local community. I would have been content to spend the rest of my career in Hollenbeck but my past injuries took their toll. Although I felt my efforts never diminished as street cop, in reality I started to lose my edge. In the fall of 1982 I was working patrol assignment 4A9, the El Sereno area, with my partner Mike G. We both were experienced street cops and our tenacity had made significant negative impact on the local gang. They repeatedly threatened us but to be honest gangbangers' courage usually generated out of a high on drugs or alcohol and we never felt any real fear or intimidation. We were on patrol just making rounds when we observed two obvious gangbangers walking southbound in a residential community, for the most part established as off limits for gangbangers.

In the rear pocket of one of the suspects there appeared to be the impression of a small handgun. We stopped our vehicle 15 to 20 feet behind the suspects and approached on foot. Mike walked towards the two suspects to conduct the search and I took the observation position. Just as Mike started to check the rear pocket area of the suspect with the possible weapon, he broke away and ran between the two closest houses adjacent to our location. We had been trained never to be out of eye contact with our partners or to conduct foot pursuit alone, but I felt I could catch him before he got around the back of the house and still be in line of sight of my partner. I gave chase and was closing in on the runner when he ran around the back of the house. I yelled at Mike to put out a description and I went to look around the corner to see which direction the suspect headed.

Just as I cautiously peered around the corner I observed the young gang member was standing there waiting for me. He immediately placed the barrel of a small caliber handgun on my forehead and pulled the trigger. I felt the hard metal hit me in the head and the click of the trigger. It sounded like the crash of two large metal objects slamming together: Misfire! I was still alive but I was not going to give him a second chance. I immediately dove to my left and brought my weapon up to fire but he was gone.

I went back to my partner's location where he had the other suspect handcuffed and in custody. I relayed what had happened and we put out a broadcast for the suspect:

'All units wanted for attempted murder of a police officer, male juvenile, Latin descent, large angular scar on right cheek, known El Sereno gang member, in possession of a small caliber handgun, considered armed and dangerous. All units be advised the suspect was last seen running eastbound through the houses; he was wearing black baggy slacks, a white short-sleeved shirt worn outside of his pants . . . etc.'

After units arrived to continue the search, we went to the station to further the investigation. The other suspect readily shared he and his friend had been walking the streets for several days hoping to have us stop them. They had planned to take revenge for our zealous crime suppression efforts and 'harassment' of the El Sereno Gang.

I realized I had made a significant error that put both my partner's and my life in danger and I needed to take a serious look at my effectiveness in the field. The next morning, due to the stress of the previous night's events coupled with my past injuries, I started bleeding internally. I went to my doctor's the following day and was immediately sent to hospital. I was advised I would need surgery and I wouldn't be able to return to full duty as a police officer for some time. While in hospital my partner Mike called and told me they had caught the suspect that had tried to shoot me and he still had possession of the weapon.

It had been a few years since the notorious wedding party assault, but the injuries finally degraded my health to the point where I required additional surgery to repair damaged and worn parts. The abdominal surgeries and repairs evidently were deemed successful by the surgery staff; however, complications soon developed limiting my ability to eat and digest food. The doctors also advised my groin injuries were going to require additional surgeries. I had had enough of hospitals and surgeries and wanted it to all be over. I began losing drastic amounts of weight and became severely depressed and some of the misdirected medical staff suggested I may be suicidal. My doctor came into the hospital room during one of my recovery episodes and advised me that if I was ever planning on having children I should start soon. He couldn't guarantee after many more stints on the operating table Karyl and I would be able to have children. Karyl wanted children and a family, so we made a valiant effort at conception. I always felt that women minimized the man's importance in this endeavor and have a tendency to take our efforts for granted. Most of my buddies at the time agreed that the conception effort should be held in high esteem and be considered at least equal to the birthing process.

After much practice we had our first little girl and named her Alicia. Consistent with her predestined personality, Alicia decided to enter this world a month and a half early whether we were ready or not. Carren followed two and a half years later. In late 1983 I had surgery that would end my career as a Los Angeles Police Officer. I was retired a short time later and to our surprise we were blessed with the news of the expected arrival of our third child: Scott was born on Halloween Day, 1984. We were now a family: a mom, dad, three children, and a family dog named Nishi.

2. MOVE TO PARADISE

Of all the memorable views, the best have been framed by
Montana windows.

William Hjortsberg, The View from My Window

After retiring from the Los Angeles Police Department and the birth of our son Scott, we moved to a little town named Kalispell, located in the northwestern part of Montana. Kalispell was our choice for two main reasons: there were more churches than bars (Karyl's choice) and there was no mall (my choice). Another contributing factor for choosing the State of Montana was they have only one area code for the entire state (still true today) which meant very few people. After working and living in the City of Angels with seven million citizens, we considered this a positive feature and it had a significant impact on our decision.

We first moved into a little cottage-style home on the eastside of town that I had purchased earlier in the summer. Karyl and I wanted to get acquainted with our new surroundings and settle in before deciding where we would buy land and build our dream home. The idea of being a family man with three children was something that was taking time getting used to. I had always considered myself to be in the warrior class: I know, this sounds like a lot of macho bullshit, but it seemed to keep me alive up to this point in my life and had been a hell of a lot of fun. Now I was into diapers, reading bedtime stories, and making market runs for emergency female items and baby supplies. Karyl tried to get me into the routine of changing diapers, but – thank God – I failed to have the intestinal fortitude to tackle the task. I would start gagging, and have to leave the room to keep from adding to the mess at hand. Karyl questioned my sincerity asking, 'How could you go from being one of LA's finest, tenacious and fearless, to a gagging sissy?' Well whatever the cause I was saved from the diaper brigade for the duration.

We finally found property north of Kalispell, near a little town called Whitefish. Whitefish was locally noted for its ski resort, called Big Mountain, and its quaint downtown atmosphere. We started building our home the following year and moved into our almost completed dream home two years after coming to Montana. We created a little family farm endowed with cows, horses, dogs, cats, and an occasional goat in the basement.

Setting up a new life – or should I say a new family? – had its challenges. When we decided to have children, I had significant concerns over my ability to be a dad. My growing up years provided few experiences to guide me when parenting issues developed in our household. We failed to receive owners' manuals after the birth of our children and more often than not were searching for detailed 'how to operate after assembly' instructions. Looking back, Karyl and I both agreed we had no idea how to raise a family.

Both of our surviving parents had been married and divorced several times. I had been raised by the streets for the most part and Karyl by babysitters. We knew we needed more information and went out and bought every parenting book, video, and cassette tape we could find. After reading and re-reading, watching and listening, over and over, we were more confused than ever. As children our mothers had dutifully exposed us to the television programs *Father Knows Best* and *Leave it to Beaver*. We finally agreed to blend each of the styles represented by the television shows in creating our version of the Ideal American Family.

Karyl agreed to be the stay-at-home mom and often declared, 'Since moving to Montana, I have fully accepted the role as personal care attendant of our three children.' She loved to garden, raise chickens for fresh eggs, and, at least while the kids were little, maintained the household and always kept the home fires burning. I decided that staying around the house wouldn't be healthy for our relationship and could set a bad example for our daughters' expectations of future husbands and I took a part-time job in town. Karyl didn't quite agree with my reasoning and accused me of bailing out and leaving her with all the responsibilities of raising our children. I justified my behavior by explaining that our girls would marry men like their father.

'Do you want them living a life with a man that just hangs around the house?' I reminded her. 'They need to see a man honoring his responsibility of being a good provider.'

Karyl finally relented and off to work I went. To be truthful I was scared to death of finally having to be a father and dutiful husband. Up to now I had constantly been trying to prove to myself that I was good enough; that I had what it took to be a man. Whether it was going to war, placing myself in constant danger on the streets of Los Angeles, or the choices I made for pleasure away from work: skydiving, flying ultra-lights, hang gliding, or riding motorcycles hell bent for leather. I never planned on living past thirty; now I was a father and was supposed to perform those duties as well as being a responsible husband. Regardless of my faults and failures in the eyes of everyone around us, we were living the American Dream. We had three beautiful children, a great marriage, comfortable incomes, and lived in paradise in the 'Last Best Place.'

We decided early on that all of our children would play a musical instrument: Alicia unwittingly selected the piano, Carren by age four made the choice to play the violin, and Scott eventually chose the guitar. Carren's first months playing the violin were agony. I often wondered how such a delicate, beautiful instrument could create such horrible sounds. But with time, frequent lessons, and the blessing of a much-needed and timely miracle, music started to flow from the partnership of Carren and her violin.

Over the course of a few short years we began traveling to Portland, Oregon, for music competitions. At the age of eleven Carren would stand tall, her violin proudly tucked under her chin, held softly by her left hand, bow in her right, and launch into a piece by Vivaldi or Beethoven that would have swelled any parent's heart with pride. I would boast to whoever would listen: 'That is my little girl.'

Thank you God for the blessing of her life and the music you put in her heart.

Carren also loved riding horses and soon became my constant companion on trail rides. The first pony she rode was a little Shetland named Mickey. Carren had inherited the mean-spirited steed from her older sister Alicia after Mickey developed the practice of biting Alicia every time she walked into the corral. It was the damnedest thing: that horse could sense when Alicia was coming outside and would be waiting at the nearest fence rail, just staring at her. If Alicia dared get within biting distance the little pony would lash out and take a bite of her as quick as lightning. Alicia was justifiably terrified of Mickey, which put a quick end to her horseback riding days. Mickey tried the same routine on Carren, but instead of shying away, she hit him in the head with a large stick. From that day forward, Mickey was hers to command. Carren would ride that poor little Shetland pony until his legs almost fell off, which eventually prompted us to purchase a larger horse for her.

Riding along forested trails and mountain meadows, listening to Carren's laughter and shouts of joy are still some of my fondest memories. So many times I have wished I could go back to those days, to those memories: life was so simple, Carren so innocent.

Our children's education was important to both Karyl and me. Every book we read advised parents to start your children off with a positive experience in the classroom. We enrolled each of our children into Montessori pre-school and dutifully participated in the mandatory volunteer programs for parents. Each of the kids loved their Montessori experience and looked forward to their next educational adventure. After Montessori each of our children attended Trinity Lutheran Elementary School, a K-8 Christian parochial school associated with our church. I always felt that our kids should be able to make great decisions if they were raised in a good home and attended a school with an environment that stressed values and encouraged and nurtured their needs. Carren, although not altogether pleased with her new school, seemed to do just enough to get by academically. She continued to excel in music and was constantly playing her violin at weddings, music recitals, and church events. So far we had successful kids because we believed we were successful at parenting. As far as we or anyone else could tell we were doing everything right.

I can remember observing others struggling with their out-of-control children and smugly thinking something was wrong with these parents. Little did I know I was in for a rude awakening sooner than I could ever imagine.

Carren completed the eighth grade and was confirmed into the Christian faith that same year. She stood in front of our church congregation and declared her intentions to 'live a Christian life, faith filled, pure until marriage, a life centered on Christian principles established by God.' We were proud parents and accepted all the congratulations with swelled pride. Again our efforts at 'successful' parenting were rewarded and we knew we were doing things just the way successful parents were supposed to: Carren was on her way to success as was Alicia and Scott.

That summer Carren advised us that she wanted to attend the local high school rather than go to Saint Pails Lutheran Boarding School; the school her older sister was attending in Concordia, Missouri. We thought long and hard about her request and decided that this might give her the opportunity to grow and mature without the shadow of her older sister hanging over her head. Karyl and I finally agreed to let her go to Whitefish High School. Carren was ecstatic; she was going to the 'big kids' school' and was going to ride a bus to and from school without the accompaniment of her parents.

3. MY FAMILY, MY LIFE, THE GROWING YEARS

The day the child realizes that all adults are imperfect, he becomes an adolescent; the day he forgives them, he becomes an adult; the day he forgives himself, he becomes wise.

Alden Nowlen

CARREN

My earliest memories are of my sister and me playing in the attic area of our home on the eastside of the little town we lived in called Kalispell, Montana. I must have been three or four. Alicia always was the leader in whatever we did and this play day would be no exception. We hadn't lived in our home for very long and were still in the exploring stages. Upstairs there were all kinds of doors that didn't seem to go anywhere. In our bedroom closet was one of those doors. I can remember Alicia warning me: 'Carren there are monsters living in this attic. Don't ever open those doors or they will get you. They will even get under your bed: So you better be careful.'

I guess I was impressionable, because for the three years we lived there I never went near those doors again or looked under the bed for fear of being eaten by horrible monsters. I know it's silly, but I still believe monsters live in that house.

I had a great life growing up. I knew my mom and dad loved me, and just as important they seemed to love each other. Alicia was the older sister and as long as I didn't challenge her position we got along fine. Scott, fourteen months my junior, wasn't old enough to put many demands on Alicia or me, so we tolerated his entrance into our world. Mom loved to cook and bake and our home always had the aromas of her efforts from the kitchen. Dad had just retired from being a police officer in Los Angeles and spent his time remodeling our house, fishing, hunting and just being Dad. I loved to go fishing with Dad whenever I could. He would bait the hooks and it was my job to keep him busy untangling my fishing line and removing fish whenever I got lucky. I didn't like it much when Mom, Scott or Alicia would come along because Mom thought I was a bit too adventurous and would insist Dad keep me on a leash to prevent me from falling in the river.

We were the perfect churchgoing family. Mom would make sure Alicia and I were dressed in our Sunday best. Scott had it easy: Mom dressed him in anything that made it easy to change his diapers, which seemed a continuous and repetitive task. After church we would always go out to dinner somewhere. My favorite place was a little café called Jason's. The waitresses were always happy to see us and I got to select all kinds of different foods from this long table of seemingly unlimited choices.

Another of my favorite places to eat was called the Smorgi. The food was already cooked and you could pick a variety of food and desserts. One Sunday Alicia and I begged to go to the Smorgi after church. Scott was about two and it didn't really matter to him where we went. I can remember going through the line, selecting mashed potatoes, chicken, chocolate pudding, pie and ice cream. Dad only let me have one. We just got to the table and started eating when Scott decided to clear out the restaurant with a dirty diaper.

Alicia looked over and screamed, 'Momm, his poop is running out of his chair.'

Sure enough, Scott had pooped his diaper, his chair, and now it was running all over the carpet. As I look back I can't believe how fast Dad responded. He immediately grabbed Alicia and me and took us out to the car proclaiming as he left that he was saving us girls from the embarrassment of it all. Mom grabbed Scott's high chair and rolled it across the dining room toward the bathrooms. Dad finally built up enough courage to go back in the restaurant and took a blanket into Mom and Scott. On our way home Mom lay into Dad about running out during a crisis. Dad just drove home and didn't say a word. The Smorgi closed down a few months later. Dad said he didn't think anyone would ever be able to eat in that building again after Scott's performance. Alicia and I continue to laugh about that memory to this day.

I never really thought about it much, Mom and Dad must have had plenty of money because we never seemed to have any problem going anywhere or getting anything we really ever wanted or needed.

The first school I ever attended was Montessori Pre-School. Alicia had gone there when she was four and now it was my turn. Mom and Dad would both take me to school and pick me up. I had my own special cubby hole to put my personal belongings in and it made me feel special to have my own little space. I loved going to school at Montessori, there were so many things to do. The teachers would set out all kinds of blocks and shapes for us to play with and it seemed they liked playing as much as we did. At the end of the day Mom and Dad would pick me up from school and before we would head home I would take them by the hand and show each of them what I had learned that day.

The next year Mom and Dad enrolled me in Trinity Lutheran Elementary School. I was now a kindergartener and was looking forward to attending the bigger kids' school. I quickly learned that this school was different; I had to sit at my desk when I was told and do what I was told in quick order. I didn't care for the structure much and it didn't take long before I began disliking school and the whole process of learning.

I did have some fun though: we girls thought it was fun to peek into the boys' bathrooms and then tease them later about what we saw. That soon turned into a calamity when my teacher caught us. Mrs Ludwig called each of the girls' parents and when she told me she was calling my mom and dad I remember thinking I was in really big trouble. Mom was embarrassed and promised the appropriate discipline, but my dad just laughed.

When I entered second grade I was taken to the music store to look at instruments. I really liked holding onto the violin, it was so delicate and I felt a sense of pride when the clerk showed me how to position it under my chin and how to hold the bow. I didn't realize then that I had just selected a way of life that would involve a substantial amount of my free time over the course of several years. I started music lessons the next week and began the ritual of torturing my family with mandatory daily practice. Alicia had unwittingly selected the piano for her daily after-school activity and was relegated to our living room for at least an hour each day after school. Dad also took piano lessons and our home was constantly filled with various proficiency levels of musical sounds throughout the afternoons and early evenings.

We had only lived in town for a short time when Mom and Dad bought some land up by Whitefish, Montana. The whole family spent endless days trying to decide where to build our new house. There were giant trees everywhere and most of the time when we would walk the property we could see deer sneaking off into the shadows. Mom was always calling after Alicia and me whenever we wandered into the forest. We would hide until she would panic; then suddenly pop out from behind a tree or dead log; scaring her half to death. We tried it on Dad a few times, but he was always waiting for us and often yelled 'Wild bear!' or 'Run, the wolves are coming!' Alicia and I would come running and screaming, knowing death was just behind us.

Dad built us a new home that Alicia and I called the 'White House.' It was this big three-story house and we each had our own bedroom on the upper floor with a window looking into the forest. We dreamed we were princesses being held captive in our white castle and would imagine a shining prince would come riding his great white stallion to rescue and carry us away. It was a grand house with three fireplaces, a big kitchen, dining room and family room. There were other rooms that we didn't spend much time in, but one of our favorites was the games room in the lower level. Mom and Dad allowed us to scream and run as much as we wanted when we were down there. That was the official inside playground and the birthplace of our favorite game – ghost in the graveyard.

Mom had always wanted a large garden and by golly she got it. Dad cleared a large area close to the front of the house; this was so we could easily chase all the deer and other animals away from the garden. Every year, after June 1st, Mom would plant furiously so that everything would be in the ground by the time the temperature made things grow. In the early summer, the fourth anniversary of our garden, Mom decided to re-enact the story of the little hen, but this involved us kids instead of little chicks. In that story the mother hen was trying to get her chicks to help her make bread. She tried to get her little chicks to help pick the wheat, grind the flour, make the dough, and bake the bread etc., but none of the chicks wanted to help. All they wanted to do was play. When the bread was finally finished, the little chicks wanted to have some to eat. The mommy chicken told them, 'No help preparing the food you don't get to enjoy eating it.'

So Mom marched us three kids into the garden to help weed: Alicia was nine, I was seven, and Scott was five. The task was really boring and it was hot outside; we were getting restless and just wanted to play. Scott, not knowing really what were weeds or vegetables, started pulling up everything he got his hands on. Mom tried to show him what not to pull up but it was no use. She finally banned him from the garden and sent him off to go play. I can remember Alicia and me looking at each other: it was a childhood epiphany. We started pulling up vegetables, weeds, and flowers just like Scott. Before you knew it Mom was furious and kicked us out of her garden as well. Scott had taught us a great lesson and it was a technique we used successfully on Mom the rest of our childhood.

As the years passed, I became quite the accomplished violinist. It became one of my passions in life. I hated the practice, but loved my lessons. I cherished the opportunity to stand in front of audiences and play. Mom and Dad eventually purchased a violin that really looked old and required a lot of work before it was playable. When we went to pick it up from this old man that had worked on it, he told me this was a special instrument and I should cherish the master who made it. He then played a beautiful Baroque sonata and then offered the violin to me. I played a piece by Vivaldi and immediately knew I was receiving a priceless gift from my parents. Just to hold and play my new violin seemed to make my life special.

I wasn't just a musician when I was growing up. I could also ride horses better than most kids. I had no fear of riding fast and one of my missions in life was to make the horse I was riding yearn for the rest and relaxation of our green pastures. I loved horses: the smell, their big brown eyes, the smooth hair on their sides and back and the soft whiskers on their muzzle. Riding through the forest or across grassy meadows with the wind blowing through my hair was one of the most exhilarating experiences in my life. Dad would saddle the horses after I got home from school and we would ride in the hills and on forested trails surrounding our home. Alicia used to ride with us at first, but she got to the point where she didn't like riding any more and then it was just Dad and me.

Dad and I could talk about anything when we went on rides. I loved hearing his police stories from days past, about Mom and him dating, and how pretty he thought she was. Life was really good for all of us then. I loved life. I loved my family, and I knew they loved me.

I am not sure why I never had any real friends when going through school. I had a lot of acquaintances but never wanted to make the commitment to belong to one of the cliques. It was a choice that put me at the brunt of teasing, jokes and ridicule. After a semester of sixth grade I started to believe what kids were saying about me. I wasn't very pretty or very smart; I just didn't fit in. I decided to try to make amends to the girls in my class but to no avail. To them I had committed the ultimate sin by separating myself from their tutelage. The sixth grade ended up being a year of hell. I didn't perform well academically; socially I became an outcast but most importantly I began believing what my peers were saying: I was weird, different, and no one would ever want to be my friend.

With the beginning of a new school year I decided I would do whatever it took to be accepted. Initially the top girls in the class seemed willing to allow me to make amends. We would talk and they would ask who I liked. I didn't really understand what they were asking and they finally just asked: 'What boys do you like?' Each of them shared what boys they liked and why. Often they would fantasize what they would do with each of their heartthrobs if the chance arose. After several days of listening and laughing they finally made it clear it was my turn to share. I told them that none of the boys at Trinity really interested me. Without hesitancy I was advised if you don't like any of the boys you must be 'Gay'. They graphically explained what that meant. With friendship I was told we never kept secrets from each other.

It was a fun game and I joined in, sharing my secret fantasies about Jeremy. I began sharing my personal secrets, desires and fears. It's hard to explain, but it felt good to have someone my age to share my life with. The pleasure was short lived. I don't know what I did to create disfavor among the female social club of the seventh grade class at Trinity Lutheran Elementary School, but soon my secrets were secrets no more. Boys in the class started teasing me about intimate thoughts of Jeremy. The stories although true had been embellished to the point of seeming pornographic in every detail. In class, groups of students would join in; teasing me about who I had a crush on, with explicit references to sexual acts and desires. I was mortified being the brunt of the teasing. I asked my new friends, best friends, how could they have shared what we promised would be kept secret till death.

Their reply was simple, to the point, and still hurts to this day. 'You are too weird Carren; play your stupid little violin, live in your big fancy house, but don't ever think you will be one of our friends.'

Their revelation was devastating. They had planned the entire scheme of feigned friendship and sharing secrets only to get me to provide information that could be used to hurt and embarrass me. I keep asking myself even to this day, why?

From that day on I decided not to try to fit in to any collection or group of so-called good kids. They could be as ruthless and deceiving as any of the so-called troubled kids in class. I would make friends again but it would be my choosing and with kids that had as much to lose as I did. I was not going to let anyone hurt me again.

I was thankful for the close of the seventh grade. I committed my efforts to my violin and horseback riding. As far as Mom and Dad were concerned, all was well. I performed magnificently in violin recitals and competitions. All I really had was my family and that is where I committed my time.

I had attended Trinity Lutheran School from kindergarten to the eighth grade and the time was fast approaching when I would be going to Saint Paul's Boarding High School in Concordia, Missouri, with my sister. Alicia and I had a love–hate relationship and I knew my life, as an underling at a new school under the watchful eye of my older sister, would be unbearable at the least. I had been working on Mom and Dad all summer to let me attend our local high school, Whitefish High. Mom and Dad weren't too happy about the idea but were at least considering the possibility. In early August they announced that they would give me a chance to attend Whitefish High. We all agreed Mom and Dad would monitor my grades, behaviors, and progress with my violin to determine if the experiment was working or not.

4. NEW FOUND INDEPENDENCE

It is customary, but I think it a mistake, to speak of happy childhood. Children are over anxious and acutely sensitive. Man ought to be man and master of his fate; but children are at the mercy of those around them.

Lord Avery (1887)

The walk down our long gravel driveway was sheer pleasure, an experience I never tired of. The surrounding forest was a mix of Grand Firs, Giant Yellow Pines – sometimes called Bull Pines – and Tamarack trees (called Larch by locals). With the first frost came the certain change of color of the Tamaracks wispy green needles to a bright golden glow. At first it took some getting used to, the thought of a deciduous fir tree, and early on I inadvertently cut down several of the trees thinking they were dead or dying. The underbrush joined the fall transformation by showering the forest floor with brilliant reds, yellows, and golds.

It was Carren's first day of school. She was overjoyed about finally attending the public high school and her first ride on the big yellow school bus. For Karyl and me, it was as if it was her first day of kindergarten. We all stood and waited for awhile, and then as polite as possible we were asked to go on home so she could meet the bus on her own. At fifteen years of age Carren thought having her parents walking her to the bus could be a little embarrassing and we were sent on our way. As Karyl and I walked back home through the corridor of fall, we each harbored our own thoughts of our children finally growing up. What would Carren's experiences be in the 'big kids' school'? Unfortunately we would soon find out.

All seemed to be going well with Carren's new adventure in Whitefish High School. She was making new friends and adjusting to the high school environment and new class schedules. She was excited about her new best friend Collette who lived about two miles north of us.

About two weeks after the start of school Carren called after arriving at school: 'Dad can I go to the football game with Collette after school'? You can pick me up at the school right after the game. OK Dad? Come on please, its homecoming, all the kids are going. What can go wrong? We will be at school until after the game.'

Karyl and I discussed Carren's request and finally agreed she could go. We justified our conclusion by calling it a school event. We broke one of our cardinal rules when we agreed to her request without first meeting Carren's new friend and her parents. 'Sure, Carren, we will pick you up at 7 pm. Have a good time.'

Karyl and I picked up Carren at the high school at 7 pm sharp. She was alone, standing in front of the main entry double doors. She appeared wobbly as she walked toward the car stumbling occasionally. The smell of alcohol on her breath was overwhelming and it was obvious she had been drinking.

'You are in big trouble, young lady. Your first venture of freedom and you blew it. Your 'trust bank' has just emptied; get in the car, sit down, and be quiet.'

'Dad I need to talk to you, please Dad – '

'Shut up Carren!' I cut her off. 'I cannot believe you broke our trust. Now get in the car. When we get home you will go immediately to bed. Tomorrow morning we will discuss your consequences for drinking.'

'Dad, I want to talk about it now. It was not my fault.'

'Yeah right, Carren. Someone forced you to drink. Oh, and by the way the school called and we know you cut the second half of the day. You are in big trouble and I am in no mood to talk to you while you are drunk. Sit there, be quiet and you will go to bed as soon as we are home.'

I was the big tough cop, the hardened war vet, the unsympathetic dad: I was going to make her regret violating our trust. I just didn't realize she already did. I would give anything to relive those few moments again. If only I had held her and told her I loved her. If only I had listened. If only.

The next morning, Carren was in the shower before we got out of bed. In her typical fashion she was using up everyone's share of the hot water. I knew that it was her never-ending life's goal to leave the rest of the family with no other option but a cold shower. I stood outside her bathroom door.

'Carren, don't use all the hot water – do you hear me? There are other people in this house.'

I walked back to our bedroom fuming. 'Karyl, that girl is intentionally using all the hot water just to irritate us. She knows she is in trouble and now we are going to pay for it.'

I walked back to her bathroom door. 'Carren, get out of that shower, do you hear me'?

No answer just hot water going down the drain. I kept the little master pin for unlocking the doors on the casing above each door. I finally had had enough and, regardless of what anyone thought, I was going to go into Carren's bathroom, whether she was naked or not and shut off the water.

'Carren, shut off that water.' No answer. 'All right, I am coming in; you are in major trouble, girl.'

I opened the door and to my horror, my little girl was lying on the floor of the shower. She had bruises and scrapes on the inside of her thighs and bite marks and bruises on her breast. She just lay there and let the water run over her, trying to wash away the hurt and shame of the rape and abuse she had suffered the day before.

'Oh Carren.' I turned off the water and wrapped a towel around her. 'Let me help.'

'Just get out, Dad, I am OK, just get out. I could have used your help last night.'

That was the day we lost our little girl. She was alive, but chose to quit living. She refused to share the horror of being raped with us, with the doctor, counselors, or psychiatrist. From that day on she lived her life as if it didn't have any value and she never played her violin again. We never had the talk I promised. I didn't know what to say or do; I had failed as a father to protect my little girl.

In my old police days we would have called in a rape specialist – a female detective who knew what to say and how to ask the right questions. Rape victims like Carren need a female rape specialist who can relate to them, ask the right questions, and who doesn't represent the gender of the individual who has hurt them so severely. Unfortunately there was none available. This was my own daughter; the thought of the bruises on her thighs and breasts haunted me constantly. I knew I should have done more, but constantly asked myself, what could I have done differently?

Karyl tried to talk to Carren without any success. Carren became a different child; she mentally retreated to some far off place where we were not allowed to go.

Carren also began changing lifelong friends. She began associating with kids that were constantly in trouble at school and with the local police. Within two weeks, Carren had been ticketed for smoking in 'Slippy's Alley'; named appropriately after the social misfits and low lifes that spent time there. Two of Carren's childhood friends grew concerned about the sudden change in her and asked to speak with me. They wanted to share what they knew about the rape and what was happening to other girls at the High School.

With what they shared and information provided from other sources, I was able to piece together Carren's rape as well as similar assaults on other young girls. Stephen was the name of the rapist. He was a six feet tall male Caucasian, with dark brown hair, and approximately 25 years of age. He had several young junior high and high school girls and boys that worked for him in exchange for their much needed drugs, which often turned out to be meth. Once addicted, he would use the kids as thieves, burglars, recruiters, and drug distributors. Collette was one of Stephen's recruiters. Her task was to bring young boys and girls to Stephen for drugs and alcohol so that he could entice them into his harem (a term affectionately given by members of the Northwest Drug Task Force).

With the help of others aware of Stephen's activities, I made contact with parents whose daughters had also been raped. It was always the same. Most of the girls could only remember a few details. They had gone to his house by choice with a newfound friend and most had ended up depending on Stephen for their drugs. Again it was usually meth. Due to the nature of the date rape drug used by Stephen – named Rohypnol, often called 'the-forget-me-drug' and the fear of humiliation inflicted on victims by defense attorneys during the course of a criminal trial – none of the other girls or their families was willing to pursue prosecution.

My attempts to secure assistance by the local police were futile. They required my daughter's presence to file the complaint and wanted full disclosure of the particulars of the assault. Yet Carren couldn't remember much, only that she knew she had been raped. The detectives wanted to know why we hadn't taken Carren in for a rape exam: Where was the evidence? Had I taken pictures of the bruises and bites inflicted by Stephen?

In the end it didn't really matter about Stephen. By the time we put all the pieces together, Carren was no longer available. We had lost our daughter.

5. THE BIG KIDS' SCHOOL

For I know the plans I have for you, declares the Lord, 'plans to prosper'
you and not to harm you, plans to give you hope and a future.

Jeremiah 29:11

CARREN

It was the first day of school and I was excited to get to the bus
stop at the end of our driveway. Mom, Dad and I were walking
down the driveway, the sky was blue and the sun was just coming
over the mountains. I was really looking forward to riding the bus
with all the other kids from our area. We lived five miles out of
town, in a rural setting and I didn't get to meet many of the kids
that lived near us because we lived so far from each other. We were
all standing at the bus waiting; I was mortified that Mom and Dad
were still with me.

I finally told Dad that the kids would think I was a nerd if my
parents were there when the bus came. They understood, gave me
a kiss goodbye, and started the walk home down our forested
driveway. I watched as they moved away, towering trees on each
side of the road, fall colors beginning to gleam in the early sunlight.

It was a great day. The bus came and I was so excited. There were only a few kids on the bus when I got on. Our home was at the end of the line and more kids entered the bus as we slowly stopped and started our way to Whitefish. I met Collette the first day; she lived about two miles north of us and we became friends instantly. She was a little older than me and was a sophomore. Not only was I going to the big kid's school; I was getting to hang out with older kids.

After about two weeks in school, Collette and I made a plan to cut school at lunch and go over to a friend of hers. We were going to party, which meant drink a few beers, maybe smoke a cigarette and just hang out. I was really excited and apprehensive at the same time; I had never done anything like this before. There was a football game after school and as soon as I got to school that morning I called home to see if I could go. Mom and Dad had this stupid rule that they had to meet my friends and their parents before I could spend time away from home with them.

I told Collette that this would be my toughest obstacle and she said, 'Just keep telling them you will not be leaving the school and they can pick you up after the game.'

It worked; I couldn't believe it – our party was going to happen.

At the lunch hour we just walked away from school. It was easy because we had open campus for lunch and when the bell sounded it was an explosion of kids, cars, and unleashed energy going in every direction. Collette had told me about her friend Stephen. He was about 25 years old and really like helping kids out by getting them beer, cigarettes, or whatever. All the kids hung out there and he was really cool.

We got to Stephen's house in about fifteen minutes. He was tall, good-looking, and definitely had a great apartment. He offered each of us a beer. Collette looked at me, smiled and nodded. 'Go ahead – let's have some fun.'

It was so cool; I never had done anything like this before. I was scared and excited at the same time. Stephen brought each of us a beer and joined us with one of his own. I didn't like the taste of it much, but I sure liked the feeling of lightheadedness that came from my first few sips.

Stephen and Collette looked at me and laughed. 'Getting a little buzz, are we little girl?'

I laughed and said this stuff really hits you fast. Before long I could hardly hold my head up. Collette said she was going out for a while; yet something was wrong: she sounded like she was in a tunnel far, far away.

I felt myself falling to one side, and then Stephen was laying me down on the floor, kneeling over me. He started to kiss me and I felt his hands on my breasts.

'Stephen, get away from me!' I shouted, trying to push him away. I could hardly move my arms or legs and I wasn't sure I even made a sound when I talked. I could feel my blouse being removed, then my bra. Stephen was kissing me all over and biting me on my neck and breast.

'Stephen, get off me, my dad will get you if you don't quit!'

Stephen just looked into my eyes occasionally and continued to kiss me all over my body. All of a sudden I could feel my pants being pulled off. I screamed and reached to hold them up, but my arms couldn't move. I kept screaming and fighting, pleading for him to stop but it was as if I wasn't even in the same room.

Suddenly, I felt my legs being pushed apart. I fought with all I had left to prevent Stephen from entering me, but it was no use. I couldn't believe what was happening. I kept thinking, *It isn't supposed to happen this way*. I wanted to save myself for marriage. What would Mom and Dad think? I cried for my dad to help me, for Jesus to help me, but I was all alone. Stephen was entering me faster and faster and then it was over.

I fell asleep and when I woke up, Collette was standing over me smiling: 'Have a good time, little girl? You sure can't handle your beer, but you made Stephen happy. He had to leave but said thanks; you were a lot of fun. Come on, get dressed. It's almost seven o'clock and your parents will be expecting you at the school.'

I could hardly stand up at first, but with Collette's help I finally got dressed and started walking toward the school. I couldn't remember what had happened for sure, but my legs ached and I hurt inside. My lips were swollen and I had bruises on my breasts and neck. Collette laughed and said Stephen had given me hickeys, I would need to keep my collar closed or my parents would find out.

What had happened? Had I made out with Stephen? Did I go too far – all the way? I had visions of trying to fight him off me, yet I couldn't remember for sure. I just wanted to go home; I wanted my mom and dad.

When I got to the school, I called home and Dad answered the phone.

'Hi Dad, can you come and get me. I am at the school.'

He replied, 'Carren have you been drinking?'

'Oh shit, he knows, Collette. He knows I have been drinking. What am I going to do?'

'Carren, just shut up and don't say anything. They may get a little angry but tell them it was just a beer, for God's sake.' She said she was going to go home with another friend and walked off, leaving me at the school all alone.

Mom and Dad arrived a short time later and Dad looked furious. I could hardly walk and I hurt terribly inside. As Dad came closer I started crying . . .

I couldn't believe what was happening. I didn't know what was happening. I just wanted a hug. I wanted for my dad to tell me he still loved me, cared for me. My thoughts were spinning, I wanted to scream, *Dad, I think I was raped, but I just can't remember.* Yet I said nothing. Maybe it was all just a bad dream. I prayed: *Oh God let it be a dream; let it be better in the morning.*

The following morning my head and my body hurt all over. I had blood in my underwear and had bruises on my neck, breast and thighs. Had I been raped or did I agree to have sex, how did it happen? *Oh God, please forgive me, I didn't mean to do this. Please forgive me.* I prayed and prayed but still felt like life – my life – had been taken from me. I was alive yet felt dead inside. I was ashamed and didn't know how to tell anyone.

I quickly jumped into my shower and finally felt some relief from the pain, degradation and horror I was feeling. I don't know how long I had been standing in the water but all of a sudden Dad was knocking on the door.

'Carren you are going to use up all the hot water. Get out of the shower and come out here. It is time to talk.'

I didn't want to talk. The water was the only thing that seemed to be making the pain go away. I had lied to my mom and dad. I had been drinking and I had been raped. I just wanted to die. Dad kept knocking and was getting angrier; I just lay down in the shower and hoped I would die.

Suddenly the door burst open and there was Dad. He had this unusual look on his face. He looked like he was hurt and confused at the same time. I was scared he would find out I had had sex and yet wanted him to know. Maybe he could make some sense of it all. Dad wrapped me in a towel and just held onto me. I don't know if he was crying, but I don't think so because I had never seen my dad cry. It felt good for him to just hold me and then he helped me into bed and said, 'Just sleep, little girl, we can talk later.'

We never had the talk Dad offered that morning. He was visibly shaken from seeing me bruised. He acted like he was ashamed of what had happened. I wish he had held me and told me he loved me. I just figured I wasn't worth the effort. The following Monday I was taken to a psychiatrist and was expected to share my soul. Not a chance. It was none of his business what I did; anyway I couldn't tell him what happened because I couldn't remember myself. If Mom and Dad thought this is what I needed, then they were sadly mistaken. I didn't need a shrink or them either. I had my friends, I had Collette and she would understand.

For months Mom and Dad continued to pay for my violin lessons. I would go, but I refused to practice or participate in recitals or performances. For some reason the violin represented who I used to be and I knew that after what had happened to me, no boy or anyone would ever think I was good enough again. I hated myself for what I had done and playing the violin just made it hurt worse. I promised myself I would never play again. Mom and Dad finally quit making me go to lessons and I slid my violin under my bed for the last time.

For the rest of the school year I struggled. I started drinking whenever I could get it, mostly from my parents' refrigerator or from my dad's collection of gifts and memorabilia. I knew he would be angry if he knew I drank his collection of vodka given him by KGB officers back in 1976 when he worked a protection detail for a bunch of Russian scientists. But who really cared anyway?

I got ticketed for smoking in the alley with my new friends and had to go to court. I told my parents I was just stopping by to say hi to a few friends and they took off and I got the ticket. I think they believed me, but the judge didn't. I had to work after school to pay my fine. I tried to get my parents to help out but they said it had been my choice to be there, thus it was my problem. I really started to hate my mom and dad after that. I hated myself as well: I knew I wasn't worth anything, so what did it matter?

6. SECOND CHANCE

If you have made mistakes, even serious ones, there is always another chance for you. What we call failure is not the falling down but the staying down.

Mary Pickford

Carren struggled through the summer, yet we all seemed to be making some progress in recovering her life. She enjoyed the time with her horse and we would often take evening rides together. Toward the end of summer, Carren confided to us that she didn't want to attend Whitefish High School in the fall. Admittedly she had made poor choices in selecting friends and she wanted the upcoming school year to be different. She had worked diligently to regain respect from her teachers and counselors at school and now wanted a fresh start. I told her private schools have strict academic and behavioral requirements.

'I know, Dad,' she replied, 'but I can do this. Besides, if I go back to Whitefish I will constantly be in contact with the not so good friends.'

We suggested she attend the private school that her sister had attended – St Paul's Lutheran High School in Concordia, Missouri – and she agreed.

The start of the new school year in Concordia, Missouri was a special time for all of us. Carren was excited: she had just received her class schedule in the mail and was already making plans to go to college. She was duly impressed by the papers from Concordia where they proudly boasted how the majority of their students attended college after graduation. Carren also asked if we would find a violin instructor in Concordia because she thought she might like to try playing again. With that revelation we were convinced Carren was on her way to regaining her life. Karyl and I hoped with Carren attending Saint Paul's, we would be able to spend some time with, and give much needed attention to, our son. It seemed that our entire focus had been on Carren over the last year and the result was the rest of the family had suffered. Scott was going into the tenth grade and admittedly needed help catching up in a few academic areas.

The day came when it was time to leave for St Paul's. We were going to drive to Spokane, Washington, catch a flight to Lincoln, Nebraska, and then take the scenic route south along the Missouri river to Concordia. The time we spent together going to Concordia was special and allowed Carren and me the opportunity to rekindle our father–daughter relationship. We pulled into the school and it was as if we were going back in time a hundred years. The school had been built in the late 1800s and had changed very little. There were still wide expanses of green grass in the center of the campus, with winding walkways that directed you to each of the varying traditional brownstone buildings: the administration building centered the campus, with the chapel, classrooms and the dorms in neat rows down each side.

Carren looked at each building, and finally asked, 'Do you think there have been other girls like me that have attended this school?'

I didn't know what to say. I just told her I loved her and that she would do OK.

Our first stop was the women's dorm where we had been directed to check in and receive Carren's room assignment. Carren was assigned to a room on the second floor and the massive process of unloading the car began. I looked at Carren and all she could say was, 'It didn't feel like we packed this much stuff back in Montana.'

This was probably true. We had made several stops along the way with Carren buying what she said were absolute necessities for survival when living all alone. Once unpacked we had to go shopping to buy the real necessities recommended by the school. I had planned staying over the weekend knowing from past experience the amount of time it takes to purchase female necessities. Being with Carren over those days made it as if the past didn't even exist. We went on a father–daughter date Saturday night and saw *Runaway Bride* and later went to dinner at the Red Lobster. Things were almost perfect.

When Monday morning came, and time to say goodbye, Carren and I agreed the time we had spent together was like the way things had been before. Neither of us elaborated on what 'before' meant but it was obvious to me: before Collette and Stephen.

She gave me a big hug and kiss on the cheek and said, 'Dad, it will be OK.' She was obviously both nervous and excited and admitted she had never put much effort into academics and knew that would have to change if she was to have success here. We said goodbye and off she went to catch up with her new acquaintances.

Carren had met most of her teachers over the weekend during check in and registration and felt fairly confident entering her first class. She had been well versed by Alicia in what to watch out for and the particulars of each of the instructors. Carren told me that one of her first classes was with a teacher with whom Alicia had significant problems and she was going to make sure the instructor knew she wasn't Alicia; she just wanted the opportunity for a fresh start.

In one of her first letters Carren related her first morning of class:

I wanted to break old habits right from the start, so I sat in the very front row. I figured it would keep me from talking to the other kids and force me to pay attention. Mr Schroeder entered right on time. He set his things down, introduced himself and then began the class by reading off the roll call. When he got to me he just looked at me and asked if I was related to Alicia Clem. I said she was my sister and he said, oh good a little Alicia. I told him immediately I was nothing like Alicia but he cut me short and proceeded with roll call. I remember thinking that it didn't matter how far or where you go, people like putting labels on you.

All the counselors and therapists advised us how important it was that Carren have a positive experience at the new school. Apparently she had made up her mind that she had no value and was prone to giving up on herself easily. We had also been advised that the school should be made aware of Carren's prior assault and her fragile emotional state. With the information at hand, St Paul's staff helped us make arrangements for a female psychologist to be available for Carren should there develop a need for counseling or intervention. Within a month of the start of school, we started receiving calls that Carren wasn't keeping up with her work. This was a familiar pattern since the rape and we advised the staff to get her into counseling. The counselor saw Carren several times and felt that Carren was exhibiting the normal adjustment behaviors of a child's first months away from home. She told us that she had advised the school of her observations and the school agreed to allow Carren a reduced curriculum the first half of the semester. The therapist also scheduled follow-up appointments for Carren to monitor her progress.

We received a letter from Carren shortly after her therapist visit and we knew trouble was on the horizon.

Hi Mom and Dad,

How are you guys doing? I hope all is well back home. I guess I should get to the point. I am afraid going to Saint Paul's was a mistake. It doesn't seem to matter where I go, I just screw things up. I am spending most of my time on dorm arrest due to failure to get assignments in on time. I really am trying but I just can't seem to get it. My school counselor had me go visit the therapist you picked for me. I have nothing to say to her, so don't waste your money.

I have met a lot of kids that knew Alicia and when they realize who I am, they respond, 'Oh yea, Alicia says you are a little bad ass.' I guess that is what I have become and regardless how much I try to be different, that is the way people are going to think of me.

I know how important it is to you that I do well here. I am sorry.

Love Carren

Regardless of the special efforts by most of the staff, Carren was falling behind in school and appeared to be slipping into depression. In our phone calls with Carren we could sense there was something wrong, but we didn't know what to do.

It seems the calls you dread always come at night after going to bed, when you're just about asleep.

'Mr Clem? This is St Paul's Lutheran High School, here in Concordia, Missouri. Um, Mr Clem, Carren has had an accident and is in the hospital.'

'What do you mean accident. Is she OK?'

'Mr Clem, Carren is OK. We had to take her to the hospital. We are going to have her spend the night there for observation.'

Whenever someone users the Mr routine in three consecutive sentences, I immediately thought, you can assume that everything isn't all right, especially late at night.

'Well, Mr Clem, it really wasn't quite an accident. Carren attempted suicide, but she is OK. She and another student had overdosed on Tylenol and other prescription drugs.'

I told them we would catch a flight to Concordia first thing in the morning.

'Mr Clem, that won't be necessary. Carren won't be welcome at St Paul's any longer; we can put her on a plane and send her home as soon as she is released from the hospital.'

Understandably, they didn't want the possibility of our little girl dying on their campus.

Carren returned home and back into counseling sessions she went. Given the events at St Paul's it was amazing the remaining few weeks of the school year were uneventful. With the onset of summer, Carren seemed to rebound remarkably and take a new interest in life. The rest of the summer seemed to pass by rather uneventfully. Alicia had attended Flathead Community College for her freshman year and was looking forward to another successful year at college. Toward the end of summer, Alicia advised us she and a high school friend were planning to rent an apartment and try their hand at independence. We weren't in complete agreement but granted her, reasoning that kids have to grow up sometime. It was a great summer and barring the few typical sibling flare-ups, the family appeared to be functioning fairly normally.

Scott, only 16, worked all summer in various construction jobs and purchased his very own car, a 1978 Ford Fairmont, two-door hardtop. His ritual efforts of washing and waxing his new purchase every evening, all summer, failed to forestall the inevitable: a much needed spring paint job. Scott was enjoying life and he and Carren formed a close bond of friendship over that summer. As the summer came to a close, Scott was excited to return to school and looked forward to the opportunity of reuniting with past friends.

Carren had a good summer as well. Once again we made several appointments with psychiatrist and therapist but to no avail: she would go to the appointments but refused to talk to anyone about her attempted suicide and the prior rape, refuting our attempts of help as overreaction. She struggled for a short time, but her employment at the Hooper's nursery over the summer re-instilled pride and a sense of accomplishment. By fall Carren appeared to be happy for the first time in a long while. She seemed to be enjoying her classes at the local college and had just landed a new job with a telemarketing company in town. We knew she was still troubled; a horrible hurt had damaged her inner soul, her spirit. Karyl and I repeatedly attempted to talk to Carren about past events, but she flippantly joked and laughed it off and informed us to get real. I know time will heal all things, but in Carren's case I felt there just wasn't enough time.

7. MY NEW BEST FRIEND

The most popular stimulant illicit drug is methamphetamines, commonly called speed, meth, crank, crystal, or crystal meth or in its smokable form, ice, glass or crystal. Methamphetamines are usually found in powder form in colors ranging from white to tan, and can be swallowed, inhaled through the nose, or injected. It is sold in small plastic or paper packets or plastic bags. The paraphernalia associated with inhaling the drug are razor blades, mirrors, straws, and rolled dollar bills; the paraphernalia associated with injecting the drug include syringes, spoons, and surgical tubing, bandanas, or a belt used to constrict the vein

Stop Drugs.org

In the spring semester of my first year at Whitefish High one of my new friends was murdered by some of our classmates. He had kind of gone off the deep end and owed a lot of money for some drugs he had taken from two other guys. They shot him in the head, burned his body, and left him in an open trench west of town. I realized my life was taking a downward spiral: I just didn't care. These were my new friends: the kids I was hanging with these days and I was willing to accept whatever came my way. Anyway, I didn't know how to get out even if I wanted.

I struggled through the entire school year; I was barely passing my classes and was on the verge of suspension due to the number of school absences and constant tardiness. The only good thing that happened that year was Mr Jim, a school counselor who took me under his wing and seemed to help me make it through each day. He signed me up for a ropes course that helped me realize that I wasn't such a loser after all. He suggested that I might consider going to a different school next year, if my parents agreed. I told him they had wanted me to go to a private high school out of state, but I wanted to go to Whitefish. He said that it might be in my best interest to consider a different option.

The school year ended and summer passed with Mom and Dad constantly taking me to different counselors and psychiatrists. I hated them all and refused to talk to any of them. I had convinced myself that I wasn't any good to anyone and that I would never amount to much regardless. Finally, with the new school year approaching, Mom and Dad suggested that I attend St Paul's Boarding High School in Concordia, Missouri. I eventually agreed with them and in August I was off on a new adventure.

When I first arrived, I was excited and looked forward to new friends and a fresh start. But all too quickly things just didn't go well. I couldn't seem to keep my focus on my classes or homework. I started failing tests, which resulted in dorm arrest. Before I knew it, I was restricted to the dorm almost full time during the evenings and weekends. Mom and Dad must have told the staff at the school that I had had a problem in the past because they had arranged to have a psychologist available for me if things started going downhill. The psychologist lady was nice enough, but there was no way that I wanted to talk to her either. Regardless of all the effort by the school staff and psychologist I just wasn't making it. I started feeling that no matter what I did I would always be a failure.

One night, sitting alone in the dorm, again on dorm arrest, I decided that I didn't want to live any longer. I hated myself and the fact that I was a constant failure no matter what I did. I figured no one would really care if I lived or died. I took over 60 Tylenol along with several of my roommate's prescription medications and just waited for death to come. Instead my roommate came in, saw what I had done and called the dorm Mom for help. I was taken to the hospital and after all the medical stuff I was told that I would be going home. No more Concordia for Carren, the kid that couldn't even kill herself the right way.

After getting home, once again Mom and Dad sent me to a barrage of counselors and shrinks. I knew the routine by now and after a short while everyone gave up and let me alone. Mom and Dad did enroll me in a class at the local community college that would help me get my GED. They suggested that after I had my classes maybe I could get a job. I finally finished the required GED course work, passed my test, and was ready to go find a job.

Dad suggested I apply for work at Hooper's Gardens, one of our local nurseries: I got the job and had the best summer ever. The people I worked for were wonderful and I really enjoyed helping people select plants for their homes. I saved my money and Dad helped me buy a car: a black 1976 Chevy, Monte Carlo SS, two-door. It had some kind of big engine and Dad warned me if I wasn't careful I would attract the police like bears to honey. It was a dream come true and my new friends from work thought I was really cool.

The summer went by way too fast and before I knew it I had to decide if I was going to go to college. The nursery closed for the fall and winter months requiring me to find a new job. One of my friends suggested that I apply at the local telemarketing company. I can remember her saying, 'Can you believe they actually pay you to talk on the phone? How hard can that be?' I applied for the telemarketing job during my last week at the nursery and was hired immediately.

I started my new job as a telemarketer after the season ended at the nursery. The place was full of kids, many of whom I had run with when I was in Whitefish. They all knew how to party and before long I rejoined the party crowd. I was also enrolled in our local college, but to be honest I didn't really want to put any effort toward higher education. Work and partying started taking its toll and I felt like I couldn't keep up with the pace. Julian was one of my old friends from Whitefish High; he noticed I seemed a little down and offered me some stuff that would keep me going regardless of my schedule. I knew what he was offering probably involved some kind of illegal drug and told him no.

As the weeks went by, I just seemed to get more tired and overwhelmed. Finally on Friday I asked for the pick-me-up and gave Julian $400; he said that would buy enough for the entire weekend. He said he would bring it to the party later that night and show me how to use this new stuff called meth. I had never heard of it before, but from what he said it sounded like just what I needed.

At the party Julian pulled out a glass pipe and put some of the white powder in the bowl at the end. He took out a butane lighter

47

and held it under the bowl containing the powder. It started to smoke and he handed it to me and said inhale the smoke.

'Breathe it deep into your lungs. That's the way, Carren; this shit is going to fucking blow your mind.' As the vapor entered my lungs, I immediately felt this rush go through my entire body. I couldn't remember when I felt so good. I felt like superwoman. I knew I could do anything I wanted and nothing or no one could stop me. My skin tingled, my heart raced, I felt like having sex right there on the floor with Julian. God what a feeling! I partied the rest of the night, I mean all night. I occasionally took hits off the meth pipe Julian prepared for me. I stayed high for over 12 hours, I didn't go home and I couldn't have cared less. I knew that I had found what I needed to make my life complete.

Meth was my new best friend.

I literally partied all weekend: I didn't go home until late Saturday afternoon. I was still high then and could only think about how good I was feeling. I avoided my mom and dad that day as best I could, I just watched TV until I finally started to crash about 10:00 pm. I became horribly exhausted and collapsed into bed. The next day was Sunday and Mom and Dad expected me to join them for church. Their position was simple: You live in our house, you live by our values. Going to church was one of those stupid values. I dragged myself from bed, I was so drained I could hardly think. The only thing on my mind was getting another hit of meth. I still had a little left in the meth pipe that Julian gave me and I went out to my car and took the last hit. I immediately felt supercharged and on top of the world. This stuff is the best. I could live forever if I could have this every day.

Even though Mom and Dad had set strict guidelines and curfews for me after I got home from St Paul's, it was easy to get around their rules. The parents of the kids I started hanging with would tell my parents whatever I wanted them to say. Mom and Dad's rules required they had to meet my friend's parents before I could spend the night at their house or go anywhere with them, but Mom and Dad never established the rule that my friends or their parents had to meet their social economic standards. I could tell it confused them when I would take them by some dumpy house or trailer for introductions.

'Carren, can't you pick better friends?' Dad would say.

My standard reply was, 'Just because they don't have money or live in a fancy house doesn't mean they aren't nice people.'

I could tell this really confused my dad and more often than not he didn't know what to do or say. Off I would go; I had complied with their rules. I have to admit I used this to my advantage. We partied at nice houses, where obviously there was plenty of financial success. The difference there was we didn't have to share our alcohol or drugs. The parents gave us whatever we wanted.

If we decided to party somewhere over the weekend my friends' parents would lie and tell my parents they were going to be home all night and would call if there was a problem. Often I thought, if my dad only knew how other kids' parents helped us out so we could party it would have driven him crazy.

I couldn't wait to get to work Monday. I was out of my little white powder and needed more. I found Julian and thanked him for the party powder and asked to buy some more. I bought enough for four hits, paid him his $100 and merrily went on with my day. I used again at lunch and again at the end of my workday.

By Friday I was using four and five hits a day just to get by. I had spent over $1000 and I couldn't have cared less. I went home Friday evening to change clothes for the ongoing party I couldn't seem to live without. As I walked in the door, Mom and Dad were watching their evening ritual, *Wheel of Fortune*.

Dad looked over at me and then took a double take. I said hi, and then started for my room. Dad called me back and started asking me, how my day was? How was I feeling? What was I going to do tonight? The questions just seemed to go on and on. Then he accused me of being loaded. I couldn't believe it, how did he know? Shit, I had meth in my pocket; was he going to search me? It must be the fucking cop in him; he never stopped being a cop and now he had caught me.

He didn't get mad or anything but he had this different look about him. Then I realized he was scared. Mom was watching me from the sofa and I could see confusion and fear on her face as well. He sent me to bed, but I didn't care because I wasn't going anywhere that evening anyway. I could handle one night at home; besides, I had another hit of my new best friend in my pocket. I would just smoke it at home!

The next day Dad said things were going to change. They were going to meet any and all of my friends before I went out. That was OK with me – I knew they wouldn't like any of them anyway, but if they wanted to see my new acquaintances that I hung out with, so be it. Dad then told me, no more drugs!

'Are you fucking kidding?' I laughed at him and added, 'What drugs? You know, Daddy, I don't do drugs.'

He looked at me with hard cold eyes and said, 'Carren you are playing with death. You don't know what you are getting yourself into.'

'Fuck you, Dad!'

Oh my God, I had said that out loud. Dad was shocked, angry and standing there looking like he had been struck with lightning.

I started to go out the door and he said, 'No way, young lady, you are grounded.'

I was out of meth by then and still had the rest of Sunday to go. I called my friends and set up to have Julian bring some meth to my house. I really needed a hit after the fight with my dad. Later that night Julian came by the house and I snuck out my bedroom window and partied until sunrise. It was a thrill to have fooled my dad by sneaking out. Now I had to get back in to my room so I could clean up and get to work. Getting to work on time wasn't my priority but Julian would be there. I knew if I went to work at least I could get a little more powder to get me through the day.

Mom and Dad set up a stringent set of rules, allowing me to go to work and then I had to come home. They allowed my friends to come by the house, but after coming by once they didn't want to come back. Dad had all my friends scared to death he would arrest them for being under the influence or something. This wasn't working at all. I needed to go party, I wanted my meth more than anything and Mom and Dad weren't going to stop me.

We fought almost every day. I didn't care what I called them or what language I used. I hoped they would kick me out of the house, and then I could do whatever I wanted.

Finally, Dad said he had had enough. He and Mom wanted me to go to another counselor or shrink (Dad's word). There was no way that was going to happen. I called my friends and told them to be waiting outside our house, because I would be leaving soon. I went out to Dad and told him, 'There is no fucking way I am seeing another shrink.' I was going out to party and there was nothing he was going to do about it.

Mom and Dad said simply, 'If you go out that door, you are going out with only the clothes on your back. Nothing else. No car! No clothes! Nothing! Do you understand Carren, nothing!'

'Fuck you, both of you,' and I walked out the door. My friends were waiting for me and I didn't care if that was the last time I ever set foot in that house again.

I was not prepared for the life I was choosing. I lived with friends for a while and then ran out of money. I had spent my entire savings, over $5,000 on meth, alcohol and marijuana. I lost my job and finally had to resort to stealing to get money for my drugs. I even stole Mom and Dad's checks from the mailbox and traded them for drugs. But I just couldn't seem to steal enough to buy the drugs I so desperately needed. Finally, one of my new friends offered to give me a little meth if I would have sex with him. Fuck, I didn't care. I needed to get high. I hurt inside and wanted to die when I couldn't get high. Hell, I decided I would screw anything or anyone if it helped me to get the high I so desperately needed.

I hated myself for what I had become. Yet the only thing that mattered to me was my meth and the hope of getting high again. The problem was that I didn't get high any longer. I was using more and more meth and not even getting a buzz. The only thing that meth did was get me through each day without crashing. I hated the crash and was deathly afraid of coming down. I had an overwhelming sense of loss and depression and all I wanted to do was die when I couldn't get my new best friend – meth.

8. METH IN OUR HOME

Methamphetamines appears to have a neurotoxic effect, damaging brain cells that contain dopamine as well as serotonin, another neurotransmitter.

National Drug Intelligence Center, Dept of Justice

Meth impacts every aspect of our community, every aspect of our neighborhoods, of our businesses, of the environment, and of our children.

Rick Larsen

My business was flourishing and the benefits that accompany success were finally becoming a reality. Karyl and I had celebrated our 31st wedding anniversary earlier in the year and we seemed to love each other more than ever. Alicia was 20 years old, attending the local community college. Carren now 17 years old, finally seemed to be having success in her life for the first time in years, and Scott was enjoying his tenure as a teenager and was glad to be back in school. It was early October and I worked until 6:00 pm that evening. I had returned home amidst the beauty and wonder of the most glorious of fall days: This truly was our little paradise.

There aren't many absolutes in life, but one without question was the expectation of me being home in time to watch *Wheel of*

Fortune with Karyl. Happiness in our home centered on the premise that I cared enough about my beautiful wife that I would share a thirty-minute TV experience with her, uninterrupted. She would watch the program, solve the puzzles, and I would thank God for Vana White. Some of you familiar with the game show probably don't appreciate Vana's technical merit on touching those letters with just the right form and finesse. Karyl said I just liked Vana's legs. How shallow is that?

I can remember Carren coming in the front door as if it was yesterday. I was sitting on the sofa. One of the players had just selected an 'A' and Vana was performing her task admirably. Suddenly the door burst open and Carren came charging in the room, chattering uncontrollably, and acting as if she had just won the lottery. She could hardly stand still and her speech was almost incoherent. Karyl looked at me with wonder and confusion.

It was all too familiar to me. It was a behavior that I had witnessed all too often in days past as a cop in Los Angeles. I stood up and asked Carren how her evening had been.

She chattered rapidly. 'Great Dad, how about you?' She had an unusual chemical odor on her breath and her pupils were dilated even though the lighting was bright. As I watched her move with jerky and constant movements, her actions confirmed my greatest fears: she was under the influence of speed. I couldn't believe what I was seeing. Memories from my police days surfaced with a vengeance: the phrase 'speed kills' kept coming to mind and it didn't involve fast driving. Speed, or meth as it was now known, was one of the most dangerous drugs I had ever encountered on the streets. It was the drug of choice for outlaw motorcycle gangs like the Hells Angels and Devils Disciples and now it was in my home.

I told Carren to go to bed and we would talk in the morning. Her face became alarmed, but off she went to her room, jittery and chattering to herself. Sheer horror must have been written all over my face, because Karyl immediately started crying, asking what was wrong with her. 'Is she on something? What is it?'

I confided in her that our little girl was under the influence of speed, a drug now called methamphetamines. The drug had become more prominent in our community. Over the course of the last year, articles in the local newspaper had detailed murders and suicides resulting from meth as well as violent confrontations with meth users by police and emergency responders. The memories of my police days in the past and meth use by rogue motorcycle gangs in the LA area and the resulting violence came rushing back and now meth was in our home.

Carren slept most of Saturday, occasionally getting up to watch TV. The day passed relatively uneventful and I just couldn't bring myself to talk to her. I was afraid, angry, and didn't know what to do for sure. The next morning was Sunday and off we went to church, our tradition intact: a family that worships together stays together.

Carren had not slept all night as far as I could determine. Every time I had checked her room, she was either sitting up in bed looking at magazines or attempting to call some unknown cohort on the phone. It had been an evening of fear, confusion and anger: trying to anticipate what to do next.

After church, I finally had the opportunity to question Carren about her Friday evening's activities. She was defensive and finally confessed that she had been drinking. She admitted she had drunk before and that hard liquor always had that kind of effect on her. I told her my suspicions and she just laughed. I so desperately wanted to believe what she was telling me, but knew in my heart that major problems were on the horizon. I would have to become diligent, always watching her behavior and her activities with her new friends.

It seemed ironic: 17 years earlier I had retired from the Los Angeles Police Department, I moved my family from Southern California to Montana in an effort to raise my children in a drug-free environment. We had built our home in God's country amidst beautiful mountains, pristine rivers, towering forest, and abundant wildlife. Why would any person want to use drugs to get high, especially here in paradise, and why my little girl?

Our lives changed radically. No longer were we just parents, we became like Gestapo officers in our own home. Carren's entire purpose in life began changing. She had a complete change in friends and activities. Her attitude toward our family became more strained and hostile. We set stringent rules for her evenings out, using the excuse of consequences due to her drinking escapades.

As she developed new friendships, we required her to introduce all of them to us and provide us with their addresses and phone numbers. We called each of their parents to verify if she was actually spending time at their houses, but later found out that her friends' parents had lied to us and were some of the people supplying Carren with her drugs and alcohol. If she went anywhere she was to call us, when she arrived she was to call us, and whenever she left to come home she was to call us. No matter how much time and effort we made trying to keep her drug free, she would come home loaded or not come home at all. Over the course of two months our home became a war zone.

At first we were shocked and filled with horrible fear; then we started the blame game.

'Karyl you should have kept up her counseling, you were home all the time – what went wrong?'

'Ron, you should have spent more time at home. You never hugged her or loved her enough. She needed you not me.'

I made the decision to confront Carren and give her the ultimatum: quit using drugs or leave our home.

Karyl cried and said, 'What if she leaves?' I was confident that if she did leave, she wouldn't be gone long. I was sadly mistaken. The discussion turned into a yelling match between Carren and me. Carren said she hated us and that 'You can all go to fucking hell.'

She walked out the door with the clothes on her back and left with a carload of her newfound friends. She was prepared for the argument, had actually planned on leaving regardless of what we said. Her drugs mattered more than her family, her car, and her clothes. We just didn't understand or comprehend the complete hold meth had on our little girl.

For over a month we didn't hear anything from Carren. The youth pastor at our church had talked to her a few times and had advised us that Carren was losing weight and looked strung out. I kept attempting to assure Karyl that she would come home soon, but now I was beginning to have my doubts. I had several friends working with the local police and sheriffs' offices and made requests that they keep an eye out for her and arrest her if possible. Two of my friends, working for the Kalispell Police Department, had enlisted the help of the Northwest Drug Task Force in an attempt to give Carren free room and board at the 'Crow Bar Motel', a local term for the local county jail.

In January, an article was published in our local newspaper detailing the horrors a local family had experienced due to their daughter's using meth. Their daughter had been arrested several times, involved in drug activity and thefts and had been sentenced to the Department of Corrections for nine years. She gave up hope while in a transition facility and walked away and committed suicide. Karyl and I both immediately realized we had a much bigger problem than we previously thought. The realization that Carren had become a meth addict was reinforced by the recent report by the youth pastor from our church that Carren had lost a significant amount of weight and appeared severely malnourished. She had only been out of our home for a month and by eye-witness accounts Carren looked like walking death. Karyl and I agreed we needed to take immediate action; we needed a plan to save her life.

We decided to split forces. Karyl was going to look into what kind of treatment was available for rehabilitation from meth and I was going to return to my old profession of being a cop. It seemed unbelievable that the person I would be pursuing was my own little girl. We no longer had time to blame each other; our daughter's life was at stake and we needed to do something now! I met with the staff of my architectural design business and advised them I wouldn't be available until Karyl and I resolved the problem with our daughter Carren. Everyone was supportive and agreed to hold down the fort.

I left the office that day and went back to being a cop. The problem was that I would be alone in my efforts. I was informed by the local sheriff's office that this was not a police problem, but a parenting problem. They made it clear I was a civilian and I wasn't working for any agency or organization, I would not be provided any official backup, and there was no liability protection going to be available for my actions. It was funny to hear those words being told to me. So many times I had said the same thing to distraught parents looking for their children back when I was a cop. It didn't matter what was said or by whom, civilian or not I was going back to my old profession and for one purpose: to find my little girl and put her in jail and I knew I would have to do it alone. Everything else we had tried to this point had failed and we knew this was our last option.

The first choice I had to make was what weapon I was going to carry. I was authorized to carry a concealed weapon by the nature of my retirement, but while working with the Los Angeles Police Department we were only allowed to carry .38 caliber revolvers. I felt I needed more firepower than a puny little .38. I had used .45 cal automatics when I was in the Navy and decided that would be my choice of sidearm. I began practicing daily until I felt I knew all the intricacies of my Colt 1911 .45 cal semi automatic. I decided to carry at least two extra fully loaded clips and kept one full box of ammo in the glove box.

I knew from past experience that crankers (meth users) and tweakers (long-time users; strung out and typically violent and unpredictable) were dangerous and there was a good chance once I entered the sewers of the drug world in the 'Last Best Place' I would probably need the extra firepower. The toughest part about carrying a weapon is not learning how to use it, it is having the will to actually pull the trigger; making that split decision to shoot another human being. I began, just like days of old, minimizing the value of the people I would be after: they were just scumbags after all. They were selling dope to our kids, hurting families, thieves, robbers, and murderers. I convinced myself that if the time came and I needed to take deadly force, the dirtbags would deserve it.

I made frequent trips to the shooting range, becoming skilled at hitting the targets at 25 yards. I practiced constantly before the mirror, pulling up my weapon and pointing it at the reflection standing, pointing a gun back at me. Over and over again I repeated the drill; finally, after days of intense practice, I felt convinced I could and would be able to take the shot.

As parents it seems we are all ready to blame someone else's kid for our children's actions. I was no different. I had repeatedly stated to anyone that would listen that Carren was only acting out and using drugs because of the people she was hanging with. As I was driving down our driveway heading for the canyon where Carren had last been seen, I suddenly realized, the scumbag druggie I was after was my own little girl. Other parents were probably saying she was the dirtbag that was responsible for getting their kids hooked on drugs and they were probably right. As it turns out I began realizing that every dirtbag is someone's kid, only that night I was after mine.

The Flathead Valley may be big for space but there aren't many people. The population of the valley is only estimated at about 60,000, yet the landmass is equivalent to the State of Massachusetts. I kept telling myself, it isn't Los Angeles for God's sake. I had been considered one of the best cops on the street in the old days, if anyone could find Carren it would be me.

It wasn't long before I realized my surveillance activities were going to involve late evenings and tiring stakeouts into the early morning hours. My venture into the canyon led me to an old dealer named Jerry. He had quite the operation and had at least 40 to 50 kids dependent on him for their drugs of choice. According to word on the street, Carren on occasion had been involved with this low life. After several nights of watching his continuous drug distribution I decided Carren was probably not currently involved with this asshole.

I contacted several of Carren's old friends and told them I had Carren's paychecks from her old job. They willingly advised me they hadn't been hanging out with Carren for some time but had seen her up near Columbia Falls; she had been reportedly buying drugs from a guy named Crazy George. Spending a little money in the Flathead went a long way in securing information from the streets and I was able to locate several places Crazy George spent a significant amount of his time. With the good luck I had experienced so far I knew it wouldn't be long before I located Carren.

Most of the locations provided to me by my developing sources focused on drug activity by teens and young adults. When I first started I thought I knew what was going on in our little town but ended up being amazed by the overwhelming numbers of kids involved in the drug culture. It took some time to finally narrow down the groups Carren was running with. The Northwest Drug Task Force explained the local drug business for me in general terms:

'There are older males, generally 35 to 45 years of age, running each group. They are the ones distributing the drugs to kids. In return the kids provide the dealers services. For some they steal, shoplift, forge checks and credit cards etc. Others provide sex to the dealer, his friends, or acquaintances in trade for the drugs they so desperately need. Many others act as street dealers at their schools, churches, malls, or in their local neighborhoods. The task force referred to these drug enclaves as "Harems".'

They further clarified that once the kids are hooked on drugs they most often do 'all of the above.' Things hadn't changed since I was on the streets. We used to say druggies ended up stealing, dealing or screwing for what they needed. I hoped I could find Carren and have her arrested before she went that far.

Crankers are overly stimulated and typically experience some degree of paranoia. It is no wonder they are so hard to track down. They are constantly moving and do not trust anyone; they were like the cockroaches we used to find in ghetto crash houses in the Seventies: When the lights came on; they would run for cover. Before long I began compiling a significant number of locations selling drugs to kids and areas where the users would retreat to party and get high. I ended up spending hours watching drug hangouts and flophouses, commonly used by these druggies, hoping I would find Carren.

When I would locate large drug parties, often referred to as raves, I called in the appropriate police agency advising them of the location. After several attempts and many arrests my little girl was still on the streets. As it turned out, it's not that Carren wasn't at the gatherings; she just had the uncanny ability to get away, regardless of how well the police raid was carried out. I started thinking if she survives her drug use, she should become an escape artist.

When I was able to find Carren it was obvious by her physical appearance her health was degrading rapidly. I had received information of a reported party at an abandoned mobile home in Whitefish. Friends running with Carren had been heard bragging about the upcoming nights events. I parked my car where I could have a clear view of the comings and goings of revelers. When Carren showed up I was overwhelmed by the deterioration of her appearance. She had lost over 30 pounds and had dark circles developing under her eyes. Her complexion, which was usually smooth and youthful, had begun looking ruddy and blemished. My police buddies had informed me that they heard Carren had resorted to prostitution to pay for her drugs. I could hardly believe what they were saying and decided it would not serve any purpose to tell Karyl about our daughter's suspected activities. It was common knowledge in the old days that drug addicts would eventually resort to stealing, dealing or screwing to support their habit. I just couldn't bring myself to believe my daughter had resorted to those extremes here in the Last Best Place?

9. JANE DOE

Life is an opportunity, benefit from it.
Life is beauty, admire it. Life is bliss, taste it.
Life is a dream, realize it. Life is a challenge, meet it.
Life is a duty, complete it. Life is a game, play it.
Life is a promise, fulfill it. Life is sorrow, overcome it.
Life is a song, sing it. Life is a struggle, accept it.
Life is a tragedy, confront it. Life is an adventure, dare it.
Life is luck, make it. Life is too precious, do not destroy it.
Life is life, fight for it.

Mother Teresa

I really didn't believe Carren was doing all the things people were saying, yet my fears for her were growing every day. In February 2001, one of my close friends on the Kalispell Police Department informed me that Carren was feeling the pressure from all the police raids. She guessed that we were after her and she was making plans to run to Seattle. To the best of our knowledge, Carren had only been using meth for five months – she was only 17 years old. How could things have gone so terribly wrong in such a short time? I had plenty of experience of what can happen to young girls that flee to big cities from my days working the streets of Los Angeles.

Typically within 24 hours of a runaway hitting the streets in the City of Angels, they would be approached for prostitution or solicited for other criminal behavior. When working Central Division one of my patrol duties involved checking the bus depot located downtown. We were to chase off panhandlers, vagrants, and opportunists looking for the new arrivals of runaways they used to re-supply the sex trade business. On any given day, wide-eyed naïve kids would venture into the bowels of the city seeking fame, fortune, looking to start a new life in the big city, and most were not prepared for the predators that awaited them.

My observations of the Seattle Street life left little doubt that should Carren head to the city the same outcome would befall her. The thought of Carren ending up in the famed University District; involved in prostitution, criminal behavior, and drug abuse brought the haunting memory of my first Jane Doe experience back to me with a vengeance.

The day was not much different than any other. My partner and I were working 1FB 44, downtown Los Angeles. It was my favorite shift – 6 pm to 2 am. That is where the action was and I thrived on it. I had been assigned to Central Division for almost a year and a half and had become known as a south end hot shot. My prior division was Newton Street (commonly known as 'Shootin' Newton'). Located in Watts, Newton was notorious for violent street crime and open gang warfare. I had made my mark and was affectionately known as one of the 'Newton Boys.'

After a brief roll call, we checked out our shotguns and received our car assignment: Another 1976 Plymouth. They were long in the front and short on power. Unlike the good old days of 1969 Plymouths, 440 supercharged engines. Ah yes, with a three-speed automatic, you could still burn rubber when shifting to third gear at 50 mph. The 76 Plymouths also had long heavy doors and getting out quickly was difficult. Not normally an issue in everyday life, but if someone was shooting at you the first thing you wanted to do was get out of that car.

We did our normal routine: 'What guns are you carrying? How much ammo do you have? Are you wearing your vest tonight?' (something I always did since the 66th Street shooting). We made up our 'free fire' names (if an asshole pulled a weapon on either one of us, we would make up a fictitious name that would tell the other partner that they could start shooting immediately, no questions asked with no regrets). Then of course the ultimate question, if need be: 'Are you ready to kill someone tonight?' (This sounds harsh but it is something you have to prepare mentally for every day. You can't afford to hesitate, or hesitate for one second, or you are dead.)

We cleared the station and announced, '1FB 44 clear available for service.' Let the games begin. We immediately received several old calls, which were typical. The mid PM shift always seemed short-manned and never could catch up on the call load. It was the same old routine – burglary reports, robbery reports, disturbances at the bar, etc. It took us almost two hours to clean up the old business and get to the important job of throwing the bad guys in jail. We had no specific patrol area; we were there to act as a floating support unit for other officers and to act as an aggressive crime repression unit. Within our patrol division we had heroin addicts, cocaine addicts, speed freaks, more winos than you could count, and approximately 2500 ex-cons living in halfway houses and run down hotels. It was prime pickings for criminals because Los Angeles entrepreneurs had started their downtown redevelopment projects and now had fancy restaurants, hotels, tourist attractions and an unlimited new supply of runaways coming in at the train and bus depots. We called it an asshole's smorgasbord.

I can remember the call coming in as if it were yesterday. It was 22:30 hrs: '1 FB 44, see the man, possible DB (dead body) at the El Rey Hotel.' God, another one! The El Rey Hotel was one shithole. It was nine stories, filled with every deviate and sicko you could think of. There were more overdoses than one could count and murders were the common population control method. We all felt that the Coroner should set up a satellite office on the main floor. The weather was warm and just in case it was a stinker (dead body starting to decompose), we picked up a couple of cheap cigars to kill the all-too-familiar odor of death.

We parked our car a few doors down from the hotel, which was standard procedure, because the scumbags would throw objects from the upper floors to hit you or your car. We met the manager and he told us that it was in room 610. We told him to show us, which was a pre-established tactic my partner and I always followed. The manager was an asshole as well, the only difference being that he claimed he was respectable because he 'got paid to run the joint.' We knew he would either get nervous or refuse to go if the call turned out to be a setup. He started whining, 'Can't we take the elevator this time?' No, stairs are the safe travel in the City of Angels; cops had been killed as the elevator doors opened to unexpected danger on the upper floors. The manager led us to room 610 and unlocked the door. He excused himself and quickly returned to his duties, dealing dope, selling whores, and collecting stolen property and of course managing the infamous El Rey Hotel.

The room was approximately 10 ft wide and 14 ft deep. There was one window, but the glass had been painted over to maintain darkness. The toilet was visible in the corner next to the sink and probably hadn't been cleaned since World War 1. The floor was slimy to walk on and the stench of death was overwhelming. The cheap green cigars, which we had purchased just for the occasion, were horrible, but stopped the urge to gag every time you took a breath. There was a single bed in the room with a single mattress, no sheets or pillows and there lay a young blonde female partially clothed.

Her eyes were slightly open, but would never see again. Her legs were spread apart and were bruised beyond imagination. Her breasts were exposed and had been bitten and bruised. Her face was swollen due to multiple contusions. There were fresh semen stains from varying time periods beneath her. She had been ravaged and raped multiple times and had finally given up her life. No identification could be found and the manager said that she was not the registered tenant for that room. It was not surprising that he had no other tenants registered in that room either.

'Shit, another Jane Doe,' my partner replied. We called detectives and secured the scene and waited. My partner started knocking on doors in an attempt to locate witnesses. It was my turn to watch the dead and make sure they didn't run off. I re-entered the room and took a closer look at Jane Doe.

She was probably only 15 or 16 years old. She had several needle marks in her arm and they appeared fresh. I counted no less than 20 punctures in her left arm. There were more in her right arm and legs. Her hair at one time had been beautiful and her skin soft and clean. She had blue eyes and beautiful white teeth. Someone had spent a lot of money on an orthodontist for this one. As much as I fought the urge, I started wondering about her family – did she have a mother and a father, maybe brothers and sisters? What could have brought this young girl to the El Rey Hotel? I wondered if her family would really want to know how she died. I started caring what had happened to Jane Doe and why.

My partner returned and said the detectives were on the way up and that the coroner would be here shortly. He had interviewed several witnesses that stated that one of the local pimps had used the room. They said that there had been a continuous flow of male suitors frequenting the room over the last two weeks. They said that they hadn't ever seen a white girl enter the room. The detectives arrived and we provided a list of witnesses and pertinent details. We stood by while drawings were made, pictures taken and assessments prepared. The coroner arrived and promptly stuck a thermometer into the liver to determine time of death. He estimated, pending an autopsy, that she had died at 05:30 hours the previous morning. Cause of death appeared to be drug overdose by others. Fingerprints were taken and Jane Doe was placed in a body bag for her next ride. We were released back to patrol and life went back to normal or at least what we called normal.

A few days later I saw the detectives who had handled the investigation of Jane Doe from the El Rey Hotel. They said she was a runaway from the Midwest. She was 16 years old and had been in town for two weeks. The pimp had picked her up at the bus depot and probably slipped her something to make her compliant. He escorted her to the El Rey, began shooting her up with various drugs, and then sold her for $20 dollars a pop until she just wore out. They said that the cause of death had been a hot shot of speed that stopped her heart. The pimp had been arrested but the District Attorney refused to file. No witnesses. After the coroner finished with her, her parents flew to LA to recover their little girl. They stopped by the police station to talk to my partner and me, and wanted to know if we had seen their daughter alive. Did she suffer? What had killed her? We told them that she didn't appear to have suffered and that we did not know what had killed her. I asked why she had come to Los Angeles. They just shook their heads and said a misunderstanding. There was an overwhelming sense of loss and pain in their eyes. Just a misunderstanding!

The memory of that family's loss was unbearable and our family was facing a similar fate if I didn't get my daughter into custody. I knew in my heart, Carren would soon be my next Jane Doe. I intensified my efforts at getting her and any and all of her drug buddies arrested.

10. FAMILY EFFECTS

Crime: *Meth labs along with the selling of the drug can breed crime,
including burglaries, thefts and even murder. Both teenagers and adults
addicted to the drug and who have no income to pay for their habit may
steal valuables from their own homes or even their friends' homes. High
on meth, there's no telling what a person would do if provoked – people
have been killed for not owning up to a drug payment or coming
through on a transaction. This type of crime requires a great deal of
attention from the police, for which a town may not have the funding or
the resources to spare.*

Drug Enforcement Agency Report, 2001

Karyl and I couldn't understand how Carren could make such
terrible choices. I personally felt I had done an acceptable job
as a dad. I had provided our children a great environment for
growing up. I constantly boasted to Karyl what a great provider I
was: 'Didn't I pay for the best schools? We went to church almost
every Sunday, had dinner at home except on the nights the kids had
sporting events and in that case we ate dinner out as a family. We
lived in a beautiful home; with each of our children having their
own room. Each played a musical instrument with private lessons
and had their own pets for crying out loud. Karyl we have given our
kids everything.'

I can remember Karyl calmly stating, 'Maybe that is the problem, we have given them too much.'

'What do you mean problem? I just wanted our children to have a better life than we had. What is wrong with that?'

It wasn't long before the blame game started again.

'Karyl, you were not consistent enough with Carren's discipline. If you had only followed up on her counseling after the rape, she would never have chosen drugs.'

Karyl was hurt and lashed back. 'Where were you? You came home, the house in chaos, berating me for not maintaining control. You conveniently made yourself scarce when I needed help and took off whenever you wanted for fishing, hunting, or whatever. Ron, you should have loved Carren more; she wanted hugs and you kept pulling back. Being a father and husband means more than bringing home a paycheck, you know.'

It seemed we were constantly at each other's throats and it was clear our marriage was heading for trouble. Before Carren's drug use, as far as I could recall, you could count the nights we went to bed angry on one hand – well, maybe two hands. Karyl's recollection on the other hand said it would take both hands and both feet from the two of us. Recently Karyl had mastered the ability to balance on the seam of the mattress bordering her side of the bed when she was angry with me or if I had hurt her feelings. I would reciprocate by staying as far away from her as possible, refusing to apologize or give in. We had often considered buying a king-size bed, but there was more space between us these days and it was becoming obvious the king-size bed purchase would not be necessary.

It wasn't long before I began considering not coming home at all. After work, I had thoughts of turning south to freedom and a new life instead of the typical trek north toward home and the constant battle and confusion due to our marital battles and our child's meth addiction.

Karyl was tired and frustrated. Although she lived in her dream home, there was no peace in her heart: She had made every effort at creating the perfect home and now everything was falling apart. To everyone that knew us we seemed to have accomplished the modern day 'Father Knows Best' lifestyle. If they only knew.

Alicia, overwhelmed by the chaos and conflict, declared she was fed up and moved out. Her statement as she walked out the door probably describes best our household at the moment: 'You people are all crazy; no normal person could stand to be in this home.'

Scott was becoming withdrawn and falling behind in school. Karyl couldn't understand how her husband of 31 years could be so cruel and uncaring, blaming her for one of her children being a drug addict. She later admitted that, like me, she had also considered leaving home. As much as she loved me, the thought of losing her child to drugs and the constant fighting was becoming more than she could bear. If we couldn't agree to work together to solve this problem, she had made up her mind she would leave.

I was sitting in my office at work, not accomplishing much when Lynn, a long-time family friend, dropped by and threw a copy of our local newspaper, the *Daily Inter Lake*, on my desk. He just stated I should read the headline story and walked from my office. He and his wife were our best friends and godparents to our three children. They had both tried to be there for us, knowing the pain and confusion that seemed to be consuming our family. Although I had never openly discussed Carren's drug use, they were obviously aware of the crisis our family was experiencing. I opened the paper; looking back at me were the faces of a man and woman with unbelievable hurt showing in their eyes.

The article told the story of the pain and loss their family was suffering. The article went on to explain that their eighteen-year-old daughter had given up battling her meth addiction and had committed suicide by placing a gun to her head. In graphic detail it explained how their daughter had participated in various crimes (possession of dangerous drugs, felony theft and deceptive practices) resulting in a nine-year sentence with the Department of Corrections. They just didn't know how bad their daughter's addiction had become. They wanted their daughter back, but all they had left was her memory. The parents' names were listed as Troy and Gerri Gardner of Columbia Falls, Montana. Their daughter Angie had been one of Carren's 'new friends' at Whitefish High School.

I immediately called Karyl to see if she was at home. She answered the phone and I told her I was coming home from the office early and wanted to show her something. As soon as I came in the house, I could see concern on Karyl's face. The prior three months had taken its toll; she was tired and needed to know I loved her and would be there for her. I apologized for everything and we both began to cry. I loved my wife and my family and I finally realized it was time to learn how to be a husband and father. I showed her the article and tearfully we agreed it was going to take both of us if we had any hope of saving our daughter, of saving our family.

Scott, Carren's younger brother, 16-years-old and a sophomore in high school, just sort of hung on during these days. I would try to spend time with him whenever I could but in reality both his mom and dad had abandoned him. We were so focused on saving Carren, we were forgetting about Scott.

One day Scott came in, slammed the door and ran to his room. I yelled, 'Scott, what are you trying to do, destroy our home?'

He looked at me with a piercing stare and asked, 'What home? You and Mom have changed, this isn't a home anymore.'

Not a home! I couldn't believe what I was hearing. I loved my son with all my heart and soul; I suddenly realized we had forgotten he needed us too. I went over to Scott and told him I loved him and that I was sorry. I asked him for a hug. He started crying and held on to me.

'Dad, is it true what my friends are saying, that Carren is a whore and a slut?'

I held Scott in my arms and whispered, 'Scott, she is your sister and she loves you very much. I don't know what she is doing other than using drugs. All we can do is love her and pray that we can get her help.'

'Dad I don't understand why she doesn't even call or stop by and say hi.'

'Scott, she can't; the drugs she is taking have control of her now. Mom and I have been trying to find a treatment program for Carren since Christmas and we will keep trying till we find one. Now all we can do is pray that we can find her and get her into treatment. I am sorry, Scott, for not being here for you. I promise we are here for you from now on.'

After moving out, Carren's older sister, Alicia, chose to separate herself completely from our family. She refused to live with the embarrassment of her little sister's actions. Alicia had completed all her applications for Montana State University, Bozeman, entirely on her own. She had asked for help on several occasions, but we were so preoccupied with Carren we just never had time. On one of our phone conversations she informed us we were no longer her family; we had abandoned her and she wanted nothing to do with this 'loser' family. She didn't call home or visit for over a year. After she had been gone several months we finally received a card informing us she was OK, no thanks to us, and in the future if we wanted to know if she was 'dead or alive,' we could inquire from mutual friends. Alicia was tremendously bitter toward her sister for being a drug addict, and toward us for obviously choosing Carren over her.

In January 2001, I received a call from Alicia asking if Karyl and I could at least co-sign a school loan for Alicia's spring semester. She was running out of money; to continue school she needed to borrow $5,000. She went on to explain that the government expected her parents to support her college efforts whether they were or not. 'Dad, they base 'my' financial need on you and Mom's income claimed on previous years' taxes. You guys make too much money and I am paying the price.' By that time we knew Carren's treatment was going to cost at least $80,000 and we had already spent several thousand dollars on educational consultants and for the Wilderness Treatment Program.

'Alicia, Mom and I don't have the money or the credit to co-sign a loan for you right now. We need the money to save Carren's life. I love you, but I am sorry.'

'Dad, this is my future. Do you understand? I am going to college to make something of myself. Carren is just a crank head for God's sake; Dad I am begging you.'

'Alicia, please understand we have to have the money for Carren's treatment; we will have no money left and we cannot endanger our credit should you not repay the loan.'

'I hate Carren, I hate you, and I hate Mom. I am going to complete my school and will somehow figure this out without you. This is the last time you will ever hear from me. You are no longer my family. Oh and by the way, you might want to remember that you have Scott to think about.'

I tried to apologize. 'Alicia, we are sorry,' but she hung up without acknowledging if she heard what I had said!

We had just finished building our new home on adjacent property to the 'White House' our previous home: It was truly a dream come true for both Karyl and me. It was nestled in the forest bordering a 10-acre meadow. Wildlife were constantly in our view, deer with their young, occasional elk would wander through. There were flocks of wild turkeys always in view with fox and coyote constantly in pursuit of their prey. Manicured grass lawns bordered the home interspersed with natural shrubs and trees. It was our paradise. We knew we were eventually going to have to sell our home but we just couldn't bring ourselves to call the realtors. We were constantly receiving strange calls asking for Carren and on occasion threatening calls demanding to know where she could be found.

'Is Carren there? She owes me money. She has my stuff and I want it back! If she doesn't call me back, she is dead and so are you!'

We put blocks on our phone to many of the numbers, but more calls kept coming in.

I was out trimming trees in front of the house, near the driveway, when I heard a car coming down the drive. I looked up and saw a gray primered Chevy Impala, 1986–87 pulling up to our house. There were two male occupants, the driver was about 27 years old, and the passenger looked to be only about sixteen or seventeen. As they approached, the teen pointed a revolver out the window. I started running toward cover when they yelled: 'Tell Carren to shut her mouth or you are all dead.' It seems my efforts at getting Carren's drug buddies arrested was having some effect.

I called my contacts at the Drug Task Force and let them know what had happened. They eventually located the vehicle and arrested the driver for various drug charges. The juvenile was never located or identified. A few weeks later I was advised that numerous threats were being made; directed toward my family and me. I immediately called our realtors. It was going to be a lot easier to sell the house than I had originally thought.

I was authorized to carry a concealed weapon through the course of my retirement as a Los Angeles police officer, and started carrying a weapon whenever I left the house. Until we sold our home, I advised Karyl and Scott that our lives were in danger and we needed to live our lives differently. We were prisoners in our own home, in the Last Best Place.

My biggest fear was the surrounding woods. We had cleared out from around the house out to 200 yards and had grass and manicured landscaping preventing someone sneaking up close to our home unnoticed. However, the tree line beyond was dense and it was impossible to see more than a few feet into the shadows. I had several hunting rifles and had them readily available in case someone took a shot at us from the shadows of the distant tree line. Our house no longer was a home; I transformed it into a fortress and constantly was on the alert for potential attacks.

The stress of constantly fearing retribution from Carren's new friends was exhausting and straining every aspect of our lives. I had to get Carren off the streets and needed to get my family to safety. Finally I called several of my retired LAPD buddies who had moved into our area. I told them the situation and asked if my son and Karyl could spend time at their homes. They agreed and I informed Karyl of my plan. She adamantly refused to leave our home, but agreed that allowing Scott time away would give him a break and take some of the pressure off him.

The only grandparents alive were my mom and dad and Karyl's mom. We had not told any of them what was going on in our lives. My mom and dad had been moved to Kalispell to be near their grandchildren and although their relationship had ended in a bitter divorce many years before, they had agreed to be amiable at least for the grandchildren. Both were in poor health and the least little crisis involving their grandchildren had prompted trips to their doctors. Karyl's mom lived out of state and up to this point there had been no point in telling her. We had advised Scott not to tell any of the grandparents anything about Carren's activities and that we were waiting to decide how and when to tell them that their little granddaughter was a drug addict living on the streets.

After receiving word from our youth pastor that Carren's health was declining due to her drug use and that she was planning on leaving the valley for the big city, we decided we should inform the grandparents about Carren. Grandpa would be easier because he was living in an assisted living facility in Kalispell and had constant contact with medical personnel just in case. Grandma Elva was living in an apartment with less supervision. I was given the task of breaking the news to my mom and dad, and to Karyl's credit she went along for moral support.

First was my dad; after the typical hellos and hugs I decided to get to the point.

'Hi Dad, we have something we need to tell you.'

'Are you guys OK?' he questioned immediately.

'Yeah, Dad, it's not about Karyl or me, it's about Carren.'

Carren had always gone to visit Grandpa regularly and paid him special attention. This was going to be harder than I thought. Dad immediately became fearful and I decided to up his oxygen supply.

'Dad, Carren isn't living at home any longer. She has chosen to hang with different friends and, to be honest, is using drugs. We just couldn't have her living in our home.'

'You mean you kicked her out on the streets,' Dad said.

'Yeah, Dad, I guess you could say that. Anyway, we need you to pray for her in hopes she will change her mind and come home.'

After a pause Dad replied, 'Oh I pray for her every day, son. I will pray constantly now.'

Then he asked Karyl how she was doing, which made her start to cry.

Dad tried to reassure her. 'Oh Karyl, God has a special plan for Carren, she will be OK. I will pray for both of you.'

From Dad's we went over to my mom's apartment.

'Hi Mom, how are you?'

'Fine son, how about you two?'

'Karyl and I are fine, Mom. Mom, we have something we have to tell you about Carren.'

Mom sat down and said, 'I think I know, son. Carren stopped by to talk to me and she looked terribly pale and has lost a lot of weight. She said she wasn't living at home and that she had been using drugs.'

'Mom, why didn't you tell us?'

'Because, Ron, she asked me not to. I made her dinner and then she left. Ron, that poor little darling is terribly sick. You need to get her home right away.'

'Mom, we are trying. We are very concerned and are doing all we can.'

Karyl's mom lived in California and was in poor health. It was supposed to be Karyl's job to tell her mom, but during a phone conversation Karyl's mom asked, 'How is the family? Ron I want you to be honest, I really want to know.'

Somehow she had sensed something was wrong. I surmised it must be the mother instinct or something. I told her what had happened and what our intentions were if and when we found Carren. She started to cry and kept repeating 'my poor little Carren.' Then she asked if she could talk to Karyl. I don't know what they talked about, but Karyl was crying. It was something special that must be understood between mothers, but after the conversation Karyl appeared to be stronger and more determined to save Carren's life.

Carren was a drug addict, living on the streets, and our world was in chaos. We were just existing, surviving, and definitely not enjoying our lives in the Last Best Place.

11. WHAT'S A MOTHER TO DO?

One of the oldest human needs is having someone to wonder where you are when you don't come home at night.

Margaret Mead

I thought I knew the full scope of Carren's drug use and had witnessed the deadly outcome of uninterrupted drug abuse too many times in the past. But Karyl had no first-hand experience of seeing someone abuse drugs. Personally, she had smoked a cigarette once with a friend and had gotten sick and that was the extent of her venture into substance abuse. But she knew, the only thing a mother would instinctively know, that one of her children was in serious trouble. When I made the decision to search for Carren and get her arrested, Karyl made the decision to find out what she could about treatment and what was available; when and if we found Carren.

The task of finding Carren was emotionally and physically exhausting for me, yet was easy compared to the task of finding out what to do with Carren when and if we found her. Night after night I would search the bowels of the Flathead Valley hoping to get lucky and find Carren. Yet day after day, Karyl was searching for some opportunity, an inkling of information that would provide the treatment Carren so desperately needed. There were constant questions: What is intervention? What type of counseling, program, or rehab would give Carren the desire to choose life over meth? As Karyl often shared, there were so many questions and very few answers.

Karyl started by buying the largest three-ring notebook in existence. She titled it 'Saving Carren.' Her first calls were to the local police, sheriffs' office, juvenile probation and juvenile court system to find out if they had any suggestions on what to do with Carren. They had no answers other than local counseling.

During one of her phone marathons someone suggested there were residential boarding schools near the Flathead Valley that took kids in and provided in-patient treatment. Karyl tracked down each of the schools and would relay what information we knew for sure: We have a seventeen-year-old daughter on methamphetamines. She was a victim of a rape. Do you have treatment for someone like her?

Two of the schools asked if she had attempted suicide and of course the answer was yes.

'I am sorry but our program is not tailored for behaviors like your daughter's.'

After several calls to other potential programs Karyl received information that a new program called Hope Ranch was taking new students. I was home during one of her phone marathons and she asked if I would call Hope Ranch while she was checking on other potential treatments. I hated office work but knew better than challenging her request. I finally chased down the number and called.

'Hope Ranch, may I help you?'

'Yes, I have a seventeen-year-old daughter on methamphetamines. She's currently running on the streets in the Flathead Valley. We are trying to locate her now. If we find her could you take her into your program?'

'Sir, I am sorry but I will have to have the Director call you back and conduct an interview.'

'I don't want anyone to call me back. My daughter's life is in jeopardy. Do you take girls addicted to methamphetamines?'

'I will have the Director call you as soon as he is available, sir. May I have your contact information?'

After several failed attempts to find out (1) whether they had a vacancy; (2) whether they treated methamphetamine addicts; (3)

how much it cost; (4) where they were located; (5) whether they had references, I finally provided my call-back information to the frustrated receptionist and hung up the phone. Karyl was looking at me with a sense of amusement and frustration.

'What? I just wanted a little information is all!'

'Ron, we are trying to find a place that can help our daughter. Don't make them angry at us on the very first call. Each call we make may be the one that may save Carren's life.'

A few hours later, John Weaver, the Director of Hope Ranch, returned my call. Fortunately, Karyl answered the phone. She calmly explained our situation, seventeen-year-old daughter using methamphetamines; currently running the streets in the Flathead Valley. She has attempted suicide once that we are aware of.

Hope Ranch is a Faith-based program and Mr Weaver asked if we were a Christian family. Karyl immediately became excited, knowing that God had finally provided an opportunity for Carren's recovery. Yes of course! Then just as quickly I saw the disappointment shadow her face.

'When will you have an opening? A few months! We don't think Carren will live that long. Can't you take one more girl? My husband is sure he can find her soon.'

Again the answer was no. Mr Weaver advised us he would call if an opening became available, but he was doubtful because they had a waiting list of several other families desperate to save their daughters and they had first opportunity if an opening developed.

Watching the drama unfold was more than I could take. To finally find a program that was willing and able to help Carren and then learn it was full was unbelievably frustrating. Karyl looked up at me and said we'll just have to keep looking. We will find a place for Carren. You find her and I will find a program.

Day after day, hour after hour Karyl made calls and talked to anyone that might have information. One day a friend called and asked Karyl if she would like to have lunch. She said she had some things to share that might help our family. Karyl agreed and the lunch meeting was set for two days later. During the lunch, Becka said they had trouble with their daughter last year involving drugs and alcohol. It had gotten to the point they were in fear for her life and had to take drastic action. A friend of theirs suggested hiring an educational consultant to help them find a treatment program for their daughter.

Karyl's first question was, 'What is an educational consultant?'

'It is a person trained to find treatment for crisis kids,' Becka replied. She provided the name and phone number of a woman in Seattle and said she had been a lifesaver for their family.

Karyl stopped by my office and shared the details of her lunch date. We both agreed that we needed help and called the consultant. Another recorded message:

'I will return the call as soon as possible. Please leave your name and number.'

We had recently received information from Carren's old friends that Carren's drug use had escalated to a dangerous level and that her life was in danger. Apparently Carren had told her friends that she was constantly being ripped off by other druggies and was increasingly afraid of being arrested. Carren appeared to have lost a significant amount of weight and appeared drained and worn out. Worse yet, she was planning on leaving the valley for Seattle or Vegas with her current drug dealer. Yet, as desperate as Carren's situation had become, it seemed impossible to find readily available help. However, within two hours Karyl had received a call-back from the consultant. Unfortunately she was overwhelmed with other clients whose kids were abusing drugs and involved in similar crisis behaviors. She expressed her regrets that she couldn't help us but did provide another consultant's name as a possibility. She advised us she lived in Spokane, Washington, which she believed might make things easier, as she lived a little closer to Montana.

Karyl called immediately and for the first time was able to speak to a live, breathing, human being. Linda's reply was the first promising response we had received in months. 'Yes, I am a licensed educational consultant, what can I do for you?'

Karyl started crying and over the next hour and a half related our story. Linda advised that she would need all of the doctors' reports, psychiatrist reports, school records, medical records involving the suicide attempt, all other pertinent medical reports, and physical information of our daughter, including a photo. She wanted to know what Carren looked like. She liked having the personal connection with the child she was trying to help.

When I got home in the early hours of the morning after spending another evening searching for Carren, Karyl relayed the day's events and that she had hired the educational consultant from Spokane.

'Ron, she is already working on finding a program for Carren. She says there are many programs that are available for girls like Carren.'

Karyl was ecstatic with the news of help for Carren, I was excited as well but I wanted to know what hiring the educational consultant meant in dollars and cents.

'Ron, is that all you are worried about – money? This is the first good news we have had.'

'I am excited, Karyl, but we need to know if we can afford the consultant, the treatment, and all the medical expenses.'

'Well, it doesn't really matter because we will spend whatever it takes, but the consultant is $300 an hour. She thought we shouldn't exceed $5000 on her services and in reality more like $3000.'

'OK, what about treatment – what is that going to cost?'

'She said there are almost uncountable treatment programs throughout the United States. We just have to find one that will accept Carren. At seventeen and a half she does not have much time until she turns eighteen and can walk away from treatment. The cost of programs varies from $3000 a month to $10,000 a month. We won't know which program or what it will cost until the consultant sends all the information and the schools reply as to their availability and willingness to take Carren.'

I asked how long did Linda think Carren would be in treatment?

'Depending on the extent of Carren's drug use it could be up to two years,' Karyl replied.

'My God, Karyl, we could never afford $10,000 a month for two years.'

'Ron, we will afford whatever it takes to save Carren's life. Whatever it takes!'

I needed some much needed sleep and knew any attempt to dissuade Karyl at spending that kind of money would be futile. At least we had found someone that was willing to help; now it was my job to find Carren.

Karyl finished sending all the requested information about Carren to the educational consultant. The calls back and forth were frequent and it became quite apparent that the consultant would be earning every dime she charged trying to find a program that would accept Carren. The first problem that developed was that Carren would be turning eighteen in July and most programs did not want to commit their efforts for a limited time. The common response was that successful treatment for meth takes time and we should be prepared for Carren to be in rehab for at least a year and more than likely up to two years. When Carren turned eighteen she could just walk out of the program any time she wanted.

During one of our phone marathons the consultant suggested we look into extended guardianship for Carren. Essentially, extended guardianship involved us petitioning the court for parental custody until Carren completed a rehabilitation program or until she was 21 years of age. The consultant emphasized that in most states, courts were hesitant to take away the new adult's freedom without just cause. The following day I contacted our attorney and asked if this was a possibility in Montana. He said he would research the legal aspects of guardianship and call me back.

The next day the attorney called and said if we could convince the court Carren was incapable of caring for herself and was placing her personal safety at risk, the court had the power to award us the extended guardianship. Karyl and I advised the attorney that we had psychological reports, psychiatrist evaluations, medical reports and multiple eye witnesses who would verify Carren's disregard for her own life and the dangerous lifestyle she was living. She was prostituting for drugs, for crying out loud!

We advised our attorney to start the process and he in turn emphasized that Carren would have to be present in court or represented by her own attorney before the court would consider the case. Fine, we would hire an attorney for her and by the time it finally got set for trial hopefully we would have Carren available.

Karyl continued the search for a rehab program in consort with the consultant and I went back to searching for Carren. Karyl had better success. She had found a program that would take Carren with only short notice. Karyl explained the details when once again I returned home from my futile search for Carren.

'The program is called SUWS. It's a wilderness survival program located in southern Idaho near Boise. She can participate in their program for up to four weeks, during which time they will conduct a complete psychological and drug evaluation. The program will give doctors the chance to determine the medical condition of Carren and allow time for her to detox in a safe environment.'

'OK and how much is this program going to cost?'

'Initially $12,000, but if she stays longer than 21 days it could be as much as $18,000.'

'Karyl, we don't have that kind of liquid capital at our disposal. How do you propose we pay for this kind of treatment?'

Calmly she replied, once again, 'Any way we can.'

Karyl was making progress on her end; now I needed to do the same in finding Carren. I told Karyl, 'Tomorrow evening I plan on watching this guy's trailer house to see if Carren tries to buy drugs again.' For the first night we both slept halfway decently, Karyl's success at finding a program lifting my hopes of finding Carren. That morning we both prayed for success in my efforts to find Carren, for our other children, and for our marriage. Every one of us had suffered emotionally over the past four months.

12. RED

High intensity abusers are the addicts often called speed freaks. Their whole existence focuses on preventing the crash and they seek that elusive perfect rush – the rush they had when they first started smoking or injecting methamphetamines. With high intensity abusers, each successive rush becomes less euphoric, and it takes more methamphetamines to achieve it. Each high is not as high as the one before. During each subsequent binge, the abuser needs more methamphetamine, more often.

Dr Brenda Roche, PhD

I had affectionately nicknamed the drug dealer whose trailer I planned to stake out by the name 'Red,' – though needless to say, affection was the last thing I felt for this asshole. Nowadays I didn't have the opportunity or pleasure of throwing Carren's so called new friends in jail for the purpose of securing information. In the old days we would let them sit in a cell until withdrawals started to set in and then offer freedom for information. Now my only recourse to get quick information was to pay money. In time the money paid off and I received information about the drug dealer that Carren often frequented. The more time I spent watching the endless parade of kids buying drugs, the more my hatred for Red grew.

I would sit and watch; waiting, hoping she would finally show up, yet dreading that she might. I chose to park on 5th Street, east of his residence, obscured from view by a vacant lot and numerous parked cars. The address 725 5th Street was deceptive due to the improbable location of the structure, accessible only from the North–South alley. The residence was centered between 5th and 6th Streets to the east and west and 7th and 8th Avenues to the north and south. Illuminating the alley was a single streetlight 40 feet in the air, atop a weathered power pole. I typically parked in a different location each time and would utilize different vehicles to avoid detection. This was the best vantage point and I hoped this would be the evening that my daughter would become the ward of our local police.

His residence is an absolute shithole, a 12 ft by 40 ft structure with wheels, trash and debris strewn around the exterior, curtains filthy and torn, and years of dirt accumulating on every visible surface. It is inconceivable that anyone could actually live here. Yet, there he is, 5 ft 8 in tall, at least 300 pounds, approximately 45 to 50 years of age. He's given up the red hair on top of his head, yet lets his unkempt remaining hairs hang down over his shoulders and to the middle of his back. His full beard rests on his chest, stained from misdirected tobacco chew. Truly a living scumbag, yet the kids flock to his door. Go figure! The one time I go to the door to get a closer look at his hovel, I can barely breathe without gagging.

Cars come and go just about every 20 to 30 minutes. The routine is almost always the same. They cruise down the alley; wait outside for one to two minutes. He looks out the window, somehow knowing what they want and how much. He steps out of the door, descends the dilapidated steps and approaches the vehicles. Money is offered and goods are taken. They are always kids, some of the passengers in the vehicles are only 12 to 13 years young, but typically they are late teens. There never is a pattern; both boys and girls line up to purchase their chance at death. So far this evening, based on the frequency of traffic and the amount of money he has received, he has distributed over a half pound of crystal meth, ice, or whatever you want to call it. At $1700/ounce it does make it financially enticing, yet how many lives has he destroyed?

Another car enters the end of the alley, headlights splash adjacent garages and trailer houses. This time a tattered blue Toyota Corolla, four doors, slowly rattles down the alley. The car is packed with kids, teenagers. Three in front and God knows how many in the back. Carren is riding shotgun. She always wanted that position when we used to go places. I can remember their cries and screams – 'Shotgun, no me, it's my turn. No you had it last time. Dad please, Carren always gets to ride up front, it's my turn.' How many times have I dreamed of going back to those days?

I've purchased top of the line binoculars in hopes of getting a better look at her, but one street light and filthy windows only allow me an obscured image. I can't recognize whom she is running with these days, but it doesn't really matter. They are all the same, strung out druggies, giving up on life, looking for that next high. She has sadness in her eyes and has developed dark circles. It appears she has lost a lot of weight since I last saw her three weeks ago at the failed arrest in Whitefish.

There's Red, as I have affectionately named him, looking out his dirty little window. He finally steps out of his shithole and I watch as his fat ass struggles down his rickety stairs. As he approaches the vehicle, he makes the extra effort to walk around the car to where Carren is sitting. She rolls down her window and as he bends over, there's Red's all too familiar butt crack glaring at me.

God, would I love to send a 357 hollow point up his fat ass. Damn it, where is my cell phone? I have it set so all I have to do is hit send and the local police will come a running. We have gone through the routine so many times before; they know the call is for real. Twelve dealers have been taken off the streets since I started following my daughter, trying to get her arrested. Yet each time she gets away and other people's kids get the chance at help.

Their conversation is short and suddenly she gets out of the car. They talk for a few more minutes, but no money is given in exchange for the all too familiar powder, 'white death,' that has become her life. I can see her clearly now, 5 ft 9 in tall, beautiful brown hair pulled back, held with a silver hair clip. She has lost a lot of weight, yet still is beautiful and still has an air of innocence about her.

It is hard to believe that she is already seventeen years old. Not too long ago she was sitting on my foot, holding on to my leg and we were shuffling around the house. She would be squealing, 'Faster, Daddy, faster' and Mom would be scolding us both, always fearful one of us might get hurt.

The transaction is taking a different twist, maybe he doesn't have any more product, or maybe she doesn't like the price he is asking.

She steps a little closer to Red and I see him smile. His stained, rotting teeth glaring out at my little girl. Why doesn't she back away, I can almost smell his foul odor from where I am sitting. Suddenly I see a look of distance come over Carren's beautiful face. Red steps up to her and slides his hand down the small of her back onto her tight-fitting skirt, and draws my little girl into his arms. As he walks her back to his filthy shithole single wide, I realize what has been negotiated.

After about fifteen minutes, Carren comes out of his dumpy little trailer house and proudly holds up her enclosed fist. She is clinching her next fix. White death bought with innocence.

I have to hit the send button now if I want the waiting patrol cars to get here in time to make their arrest. Yet all I can do is sit and watch as the dirty little Toyota slowly pulls down the alley, taking Carren, my little girl, away from me one more time. Tears stream down my face and I feel as if my heart is being torn from chest. What has happened to my little girl, where has she gone?

I began having chest pains as I sat in my car watching Carren leave Red's and disappear down the alley. I couldn't catch my breath and the pain in my chest was so intense I could hardly breathe. I lay back in my seat and just tried to relax in hope that the excruciating pain would go away. I remember praying: *God let me die here and now; I just can't take anymore. Please let me die.*

I woke up several hours later; I knew I hadn't gone to heaven because there was Red's shithouse trailer. It was daylight and I was hurting all over. I called my doctor and she had me go to the hospital. Once they had plugged me into a few machines, things started getting exciting. Evidently, my heart rate was crazy and the next thing I knew I was in a cardio unit with the doctors and nurses attempting to stabilize my heart rate.

13. HITTING BOTTOM

*Like people with secret, shameful lovers, addicted people hide their
addictions from themselves and from everyone else who might separate
them from their lovers. Their behavior continues despite the pain these
abusive love affairs produce. Addiction turns love and pleasure, natural
processes, into nightmares because of the inescapable long-term negative
consequences of the addicted brain's chemical love affair*

Dr Robert Dupont, The Selfish Brain

CARREN

When I first started using meth I felt like I was superwoman. I
had no idea how short a time that feeling would last. Two of
my friends and I decided to party in a little town north of Kalispell,
called Columbia Falls.

Columbia Falls had a reputation for being a party town. What
made it great was there were only three cops in the entire town and
we could pretty much party without interruption. We checked in to
a cheap little dirty hotel room, bought some beer, and made
ourselves comfortable.

When Jon, the supplier arrived, he began to break out the meth
and everything that would be necessary to use it. He started

unpacking all of these funny utensils; the tubing of a pen, a light bulb, some salt and this funny white stuff. He dissected the light bulb carefully as he instructed us on how important it is to do this just right. He poured salt into the glass portion of the bulb, covered the top and then shook it vigorously. I asked what he was doing that for and his reply was quick and to the point.

'If you don't get all the coating off the inside of the bulb, it creates a toxin that can make you deathly sick or even kill you.'

Here we were, worrying about toxic lining of a light bulb and the real death was in the little white powder (meth) that we were intentionally going to put back in the bulb, melt to a vapor, and then inhale into our lungs. Once the bulb was clear, a single white rock was placed in the bulb and slowly melted using a small cigarette lighter. The whole process became entrancing! I was told to hold the pen in my mouth between my teeth when I breathed in or the smoke would kill my teeth. It should have crossed my mind: What am I doing breathing in chemicals that will rot my teeth, are poison and contain toxic gasses? I had concerns but not enough to stop what I was doing.

The dealer held the dismantled light bulb for me and told me to breathe in and twist the bulb, breathing in continually. He explained each detail of what I needed to do to get high with his technique in using meth. I remember thinking that this was too complicated and that I would only do crystal meth just once.

Before those thoughts had time to register, the high hit me like a freight train. It was just fractions of a second since I had inhaled my first breath of this strange smoke and I could feel this wave of pleasure rushing through my body. Any doubts I had before were gone. I was now fearless and felt totally in control. I felt like superwoman and knew I was invincible.

We smoked rock after rock, only taking short breaks to drink the beer we had brought along. The alcohol meant little, but the pause helped build the anticipation for my next hit on the light bulb. Next we tried using the meth by sniffing it into our nose. The dealer brought out a mirror and put several of the rock chunks on it. He then began cutting it with his plastic credit card. When it was fine enough he arranged it into lines and passed me a straw.

'Hold this in one side of your nose and close the other side with a finger.' he said. 'Then breathe in and inhale the line of powder up your nose.'

This was called snorting. We tried this technique a couple of times and the burning in my nose was almost unbearable. The chemicals drained from my nose to the back of my throat and I felt like I was drinking a foul cough syrup or some chemical from under the kitchen sink. I immediately chased the line with a beer to drown out the foul flavor. Regardless of the taste, or the sick feeling caused by the chemicals in my throat, the high that followed made it all worth it.

Once again I felt like superwoman and there wasn't anything I couldn't do. I partied all night with my friends, could drink continuously without getting drunk, and danced every dance. I just knew everyone thought I was the life of the party. The high was so intense; it was unbelievable. I had unlimited energy, my skin flushed then tingled and I felt as if someone was gently rubbing my entire body all at once, and I had this glowing feeling inside that just made me feel like I could soar through the sky. I felt good inside for the first time since I could remember. I know I spent at least $400 to $500 dollars that weekend on meth and I would have easily spent ten times that amount for that feeling.

What was amazing is how short the good feeling lasted. After using for about a month, I just wasn't getting as high. I started using more alcohol and other drugs with the meth just to get a buzz or to avoid the crash. I had to use more and more to get a high feeling, yet it was never as good as I remembered. The really horrible experience was the lows. When I came off meth I was so tired I could hardly move. I felt like the whole world was crushing down on me. I felt dirty, I couldn't remember what I had done the night before and there was this never-ceasing sense of gloom. The only thing I could think about was getting my next fix.

The method I preferred for using meth was smoking it out of a piece of folded tin foil, called a 'foily.' The foil was folded almost like an airplane and when it swirled off the surface it was mesmerizing. The high was also intense when you used meth that way. Other kids started injecting in their veins when smoking didn't give them the high feeling anymore. I hated needles, but I was almost at the point I would try anything to make this horrible feeling of gloom and fatigue go away.

I knew my dad was catching on to my drug use when he asked me to give him a ride to work in the morning. Sheer panic set in! How was I going to hide the evidence of my daily drug use? My car had become an extension of who I was and what I was doing. I had learned how to heat meth on pieces of tin foil and now kept a ready supply under the seat of my car. The straws I used for sucking up the precious fumes were stored in my glove box. I wonder what the fast food restaurants would think knowing we used them repeatedly for our supply of straws: 'Yes, a glass of water with extra straws please.'

Many times I needed my high so desperately I would get careless and burn the car seats. When Dad first found my car it was immaculate and I knew he would notice the burns immediately. More telling was the smell; the burning meth we used created an odor similar to cat urine. Dad used to tell me stories when he worked narcotics and how they would find druggies by the smells they left behind. My only chance of keeping Dad from finding out was to have Scott drive Dad to work the next morning. When I asked him, he refused instantly.

'You take him, Carren, he asked you not me. What is so hard about it anyway, that's the way you go to work.'

'Scott, you know Dad hates my job at the telemarketing place, he constantly lectures me about it here at home. I don't want to hear the same old speech all the way to work'

There was no way I could tell Scott why I didn't want Dad in my car so I resorted to begging him. Again he refused and asked why it was so important and what was I afraid of? I finally shared that I had been partying all night and if Dad rode in my car he would find out. Scott just laughed and refused all the same. I decided the only way to keep my new life with meth a secret would be to clean my car completely.

I got up at 4:30 that morning and started cleaning. First, I disposed of all the tin foil, threw away all the straws, and then dumped a half bottle of perfume on the seats and carpets. When Dad and I were finally ready to go I was sure I had done a good job. As he entered my car I realized all my efforts had been for naught. Dad just looked at me with a look of anger and sadness all at the same time. He knew, now what?

I knew I couldn't live at home and use my drugs. Mom and Dad had put me essentially under house arrest and the only thing that seemed to matter to me now was smoking my next 'foily' of meth. I told my friends to come pick me up at my house and then started an argument with my parents. They told me that using drugs and alcohol were not permitted in their home and if I was not willing to live by their rules I would have to move out. I fought back by arguing that I was already living the life of an adult and so I was going to enjoy the privileges of one.

Ultimately I knew they were going to persist in the ultimatum; my plan had worked. I walked out of their lives, away from my brother, my sister, and my car; gave up all my possessions, my memories, and walked out of my home. They were no longer part of my life nor was I planning on being part of theirs.

It wasn't long before I ran out of money. Living on the streets was more expensive than I had expected. I had saved up almost $5000 from working at Hooper's Nursery and now it was all gone – sucked up my nose through plastic straws and burned up on my tin foil. At first my dealers would give me some free stuff every now and then when I ran short of cash, but soon they expected me to give them something back. All I had left was my body; I needed my meth desperately and willingly traded myself for my next high. It wasn't long before my body wasn't enough to get the meth I so desperately needed. I would have to move on to a new group of friends for a place to stay and my next high.

When I first started hanging around with my new friends, we almost never had any contact with the police. Now, it seemed wherever I went the police were constantly showing up and making arrests. We constantly had to keep changing where we were having our parties, where we were sleeping, and where we went to break into cars and houses for fear of getting arrested.

One evening we were all partying in an old locked down trailer in Whitefish. We had broken the rear window to get in and during the process woke the neighbors.

'What are you kids doing over there?' the neighbor yelled out.

We came up with some phony story and told them to go back to bed or we would be over there next. Meth seemed to take away any fears we had and most of the people who weren't part of our group avoided us at all costs. The party was just getting started and all of us were pretty high.

Suddenly I started feeling uneasy and had this feeling someone was after me. I knew I had to get out of this place and in a hurry. I decided to use the excuse of making a food run and asked if anyone was hungry. There was a cheap chain restaurant down the road, one of the employees partied with us on occasion and we knew he would give us free food as long as we gave him what he wanted. I guess you could have called it a barter system of sorts. Typically we traded what we had available which was ourselves.

The ride there was a blur. I was driving some kid's Mustang because he was too loaded to drive. I kept thinking, he was too loaded; I couldn't remember how to get to the restaurant, let alone drive a car. Shortly after arriving at the restaurant several of the kids from the party came clamoring in and slid into the booth with us. They were chattering a mile a minute about how the cops had raided the trailer and a couple of people were arrested.

After several more arrests I started making plans to go to Seattle. Paranoia seemed to be my constant companion and I knew I needed to get out of the Flathead Valley. I had several friends I had met over the last couple of months who had moved over to the city. They said it was easier to get your dope and if you played your cards right you could make all the money you needed plus some. I had to get enough money saved up to pay for the trip, or find someone who would take me for what I had to offer. In the mean time I just kept moving around from group to group, friend to friend.

I met one of my new, so-called 'boyfriends' at one of our group parties. He was from a little town near Glacier Park, named West Glacier. He had recently moved to Kalispell and was paying weekly for a room in a motel south of town. It was a pretty nice place and it was nice to have a warm bed, clean sheets, and food for a change. We were both using meth and each other. He seemed content with me and I definitely was happy with my new accommodations.

We had heard there was supposed to be a great party that evening and we both planned to go. I don't remember what day it was, and it didn't really matter. My life revolved around the next party, the next high, and all too often waking up in strange surroundings. At least this morning I knew where I was. I woke up and began my usual routine, when conditions allowed. I got into the shower and turned the water as hot as I could stand it: I would wash my hair three times, my face twice and my body over and over. I could almost wash away the hurt and filth that seemed to be part of me these days. I wanted to look perfect for the big night out and was spending extra time putting on my makeup.

As I looked in the mirror I suddenly realized I didn't know the person looking back at me. The eyes had lost any indication of life or joy. The youthful face had vanished; there was just a tired, scared, and worn out woman that just kept asking 'why'? The life I had chosen had left me empty and lost. The face looking back at me realized she had no future and had given up a great life for meth.

I kept telling myself that it didn't matter because I had achieved the ultimate goal; I was out on my own, enjoying the freedom from Mom and Dad. My new friend had taken away most of the painful memories and no one could hurt me again; that much I could count on. Yet, when I looked back at my reflection, I realized for the first time I was scared. I was looking at something dark and evil. I began to confuse the lies I told myself with the truth. I couldn't believe how, in a few short months, I had gone from Mom and Dad's little girl to the person that was looking back at me today.

The party went as usual: there was a lot of alcohol, lots of drugs and eventually turned into another night of 'fun.' The next morning I woke up next to my new current 'boyfriend.' I forced myself to go to work when he went into town. I had managed to keep my job at the telemarketing place, but for how much longer I wasn't sure: Most of the time I was late or didn't show up at all. A couple of friends came by my work; I arranged for them to pick me up at the end of the day.

Getting around was becoming a problem. I didn't have a car; many of my friends were in jail or had just disappeared. I constantly had to keep finding someone I could bum a ride with. I was planning to go to my new home with my friend from West Glacier where I could clean up and get ready to go out and party again. My friends were evasive and hesitant to take me to my new, best home.

Finally I got pissed off and asked what was going on.

'Your new 'boyfriend' has some other girl at his place. He doesn't want you back there.'

'Yeah, whatever!'

I didn't believe, or maybe couldn't believe, what they were saying. Is that what I had become? A person to be used and discarded when something better came along. I had to find out if what they were saying was true. They finally agreed to take me out to his house; he had in fact replaced me with someone else. When I asked what the hell was going on, he just replied, 'That's the way things are.'

I felt hurt and betrayal and realized I had no value. Not to him, not to me, and not to anyone else.

I left with my friends and once again used my new best friend to take away the pain. The high was so great; I could stand another day of life. We found another party that night and I ran into my old, new boyfriend. I wanted him to know what he was missing by giving me up. He couldn't have cared less. Once again I was without a place to stay. I felt lost and discarded. I remembered the face I had seen in the mirror that morning and started to cry.

Regardless of how much I smoked or drank, I had this horrible sense of loneliness. Something inside of me snapped. I ran outside, down the street and away from the party. What the hell was going on? I had no more meth and no place to stay, I was ashamed of who I was, of what I had become, and decided to end my life. I took out a bottle of pills I had stolen from a car earlier that evening. I didn't know exactly what they were, but I swallowed all of them. I sat down and waited for life to be over. I didn't want to face another day.

I don't know how I survived, but I woke up in another strange house with yet another group of so-called friends. I couldn't believe I was alive: I couldn't even kill myself the right way. I knew the routine pretty well by now. I couldn't remember how many times I had woken up in places I didn't recognize. The new group would accept me as long as they knew I was one of them. Most of them were out of money as well, and resorted to breaking into cars to finance their existence. They were willing to help me out, but I just had to give them something back in return. Again, all I had left was me and for now that was good enough.

With a little training and practice I became quite good at removing stereos from cars. In less than five minutes I could take the entire system out from under the dash and remove speakers or anything else that was in the car. People in town were so stupid; they never locked their cars and women would leave their purses tucked under the seats just for the taking. The best place for scoring was in Whitefish. It was the tourist part of our valley; people had lots of money. It seemed ironic: that is where a few short months ago I had chosen to go to high school, what I had called 'the big kids' school.' Now I was going there to rip off cars, steal purses, or take whatever I could to purchase my next high.

We never got a lot of money for the stuff we stole. The dealers most of the time ripped us off, either by stealing from us or giving us bad stuff (home-cooked meth) in exchange for our efforts. I was constantly arguing with them about how we weren't able to trust them. I remember thinking as we left the dealer with our next high in our pockets: trust, what a joke; my dad would have laughed himself silly if he heard me using that phrase.

We had been ripping off cars for several days and finally I had enough cash to buy the next hook up. The one asshole that always had plenty of meth was Red. I hated the guy with all my heart, but if we wanted another chance at heaven, he had the stuff. I gave him a call and set up the buy. He lived in a filthy little house trailer just west of Flathead High School in downtown Kalispell. Typically, you just drove up the alley and he would come out, take your money, give you the stuff and you would be on your way.

For some reason he was nervous about making the deal in the alley next to his house. He told me I had to come in to make the transaction. He was this fat ass, and weighed about three hundred pounds. He had long red hair on the sides of his head and was bald on top. When he chewed tobacco he drooled and had dark tobacco stains on his red straggly beard. I was afraid of him, but nevertheless, I wanted, I needed, my high desperately.

We pulled up the alley and I got out of the passenger side of the car. There was fat ass Red, he walked out of the trailer and met me halfway.

'Let's go inside, darlin',' he said, and then reached down and grabbed my ass.

'Fuck you, Red, I got the money, you got the shit?'

'Yeah inside, come on in. My friends just watched from the car. They were afraid of Red as well. His house stunk of smoke, moldy food and sweat from his fat ass.

'Hey girl you want this stuff for free? I can help you out.'

'Fuck you Red, just get me the shit, I told you I have money.'

He screwed around for the longest time, bagging up this funny-colored crystal powder shit.

'Red, is this stuff good? I can't waste my money on bad shit?'

'It's OK. The other kids are OK with it; you getting too uppity to use my shit, missy?'

'Just give it to me.'

I paid him the money and left his stinking shithole house. As I walked back to the car my friends looked concerned that maybe I didn't score or thought I had used their money to get high inside. I held up my hand in triumph, another high for each of us and off we went to party.

I can remember smoking the pipe of stuff from Red and it burned green. Back in the old days, just a few short months ago, my old dealers told me never to smoke the shit if it burned green or blue: It was bad stuff and would kill you. I didn't care. I had been out for three nights stealing anything and everything I could to raise the fifty dollars I spent on this high. If it killed me, so be it, I was willing to take the chance to get high one more time. I got sick instantly. My heart was racing, and I felt like my face was on fire. It felt like my skin was crawling from my body and like my head was going to explode. I don't remember what happened the rest of the night.

I woke up lying on the floor, on a filthy carpet with trash and beer cans all around me, in a dirty little room, in another filthy singlewide trailer. I was so sick I just prayed to God that I would die. I hadn't eaten in over three days, I couldn't remember the last time I had had a bath or shower. I couldn't remember the names of the people I was even hanging with. I wanted to go home, but I refused to give in to my dad. He could be such an asshole and I wasn't going to give him the pleasure of telling me, 'I told you so. I knew you couldn't make it living on your own.'

For a brief moment I thought of calling Mom – maybe she'd help me out? I just needed a little money to get me by. No, Dad would find out and stop her. She always told him everything anyway. I decided to call Brad, the youth pastor at our church. He seemed like he cared about me and had always been there to listen when I needed someone to talk to over the last couple of months.

Brad answered the phone and asked how I was doing.

'I'm not so good, Brad. I just had a bad night and I am hungry, sick, and don't know what to do.'

He said he would meet me at Finnegan's restaurant and buy me something to eat. I told him I couldn't get there until around 11 am and we agreed to meet.

Brad bought me lunch and we sat there and made small talk for a while. He finally told me I looked horrible and needed help.

'I'm OK. I will make it.'

'Carren, your dad is in the hospital; he had a heart attack last night.'

'I don't really care,' I replied. 'He doesn't care about me anyway.'

'Carren, you don't believe that. He loves you more than you will probably ever know. Anyway, you should at least go by and see him. You wouldn't want him to die without at least saying goodbye.'

I didn't answer. We continued to talk as I ate. I was so tired and the food was making my stomach hurt. I felt like I was going to throw up and wanted to get away from all the people, away from Brad.

'I got to go, Brad, thanks for the help, for being there.'

I couldn't believe my dad was in the hospital and he could possibly die. In my heart I knew it was my fault, yet the thought of actually seeing him again scared me to death. He seemed to be able to look right through me and know what I was thinking, what I had been doing. In the old days I could never lie to him because he would look at me and I would just start crying and tell all. He wasn't so strong now; maybe I would go by and see him.

I caught a ride to the hospital with two of my new friends. I didn't have clean clothes to wear, but I cleaned up as best I could. I walked up to the information desk and stood there for a moment without saying anything.

'Is there anything I can do for you, miss?'

I asked the lady for the room number of my dad, giving his name. She looked at me, at my clothes, my face, and sadness seemed to shadow her face.

'Are you family?'

'Yeah, I told you, I am his daughter.'

I hate it when people pity me, and I almost felt like that was exactly what she was doing, even though she didn't even know who I was. Yet, she also had the kindest eyes and seemed to be genuinely concerned.

'He is in critical care,' she explained. 'You will need to check in with the nurses at the desk before you go in.'

I thanked her and as I walked away I remember thinking, maybe she wasn't that bad. My friends and I took the elevator up to the second floor. I checked in at the nurses' station, giving my dad's name. The duty nurse looked challengingly at my friends and repeated the now familiar statement that family members only could visit. I repeated the same story as before: 'I am his daughter.'

She nodded and pointed me to Dad's room. I walked slowly down the hall, trying to see into the room without him seeing me first. I peeked inside the door and thank God he was asleep. He had wires coming from everywhere and was really pale. It was so weird, he always seemed so strong, now he was just an old man and very sick. He looked like he had aged a hundred years since I had seen him five months ago. His hair was almost completely gray and he seemed to have lost a lot of weight.

I started to cry. I wanted to reach down and kiss his cheek, but I was afraid. I was so dirty; I had done so many things that had hurt him, that had hurt my whole family. I turned away and wiped the tears from my face. As I turned back around, my dad's eyes were open and he was staring at me. His stare was intense, yet he seemed to be telling me, I love you little girl. I just looked at him for a moment and then he asked me for a hug.

Thoughts were racing through my head. *God no, I can't do that. I'm filthy, I'm so dirty, and I'm not his little Carren any longer.*

I could feel the tears welling up inside me. I was going to burst into tears if I didn't get out of there. I didn't say a word; I just looked down at Dad and shook my head – no, and walked away. As I walked by the nurses' station I could hear alarms and beeping sounds going off. They had their problems and I had mine.

14. DEATH: HER ONLY CHOICE

Dear Mom and Dad,
Help me! I am chemically dependent. I will not admit my addiction to you
– you will have to admit to my addiction for me. I make excuses for my
self-destructive behavior – please don't believe them. I ignore reality – I
hope you won't. I have lied to you, stolen from you, hurt you in many
ways – please separate my actions from myself. I will try to get you to act
out of anger – please respond out of care. I have lost my faith – please
pray for me. I do not love myself – please love me. I need help – please
find it for me.
If I could be honest I would write you this letter. However, you need to
know that my addiction to meth will not allow such honesty. Please learn
all you can and help me. I am dying.

> Anonymous drug users' collective reflections
> on what they would have told their family

K aryl received the call from our doctor that I was in the hospital. They just told her I had some issues with my heart and she should come to the hospital. My night with Red had not gone well, even though I had actually seen Carren. Karyl walked into my room. She first glanced at me, then at all the wires and machines monitoring every function of my life. I always loved watching Karyl walk into a room. Deep blue eyes, as beautiful as the day we were married. What had it been – 32 years ago we started our lives together.

She gave me a kiss and asked, 'How you doing?'

'Oh I'm OK; I am just a little tired that's all.'

'The doctors say you have given your heart a little too much stress.'

'Karyl, I saw Carren last night at Red's. I should have called the police but I didn't: I just cried. She isn't doing very well; she has lost a tremendous amount of weight and has terrible circles under her eyes. She looks ten years older than she is!'

Karyl asked where I had seen her.

'At Red's,' I replied. 'She was buying dope,' I thought without saying, well kind of buying dope. 'She was with some other kids. It hurt so bad to see her in the condition she was in I just started crying. I don't think she is going to live much longer and I now I don't think I will be able to chase her any more'.

It is okay Ron; let's just get you well and out of here. The doctor said you needed rest. I will come back this afternoon and see how you are doing. I love you and don't worry about Carren. God will take care of her.'

Karyl hadn't seen how far downhill Carren had gone and I wasn't sure if God took time out of his day to be at places like Red's. For now I knew there was nothing I could do. I was stuck in the hospital and Carren was still running the streets.

My second day in the hospital involved test, rest and more tests. Apparently I had not slept enough, had way too much stress, and it had taken its toll on my heart. In the future I needed rest, lots of rest according to the doctor, and tender loving care to recover. Karyl had been in that morning to visit before going off to her daytime job. I was relegated to bed most of the time. My thoughts kept going back to a couple of nights past and seeing Carren with Red.

I had been in the hospital a couple of days and was recovering. Karyl was by my side. She looked beautiful and scared at the same time. I told her that I couldn't chase Carren any longer. I shared what I had seen a few nights before at Red's. We were both crying and I said, 'I don't think we can save Carren. Meth has control of our little girl now, she can't live much longer.'

I had made up my mind that I would probably never see Carren alive again.

Left: Carren, Alicia and Scott living life to its fullest, a true picture of innocence, in the "Last Best Place."

Below: We were blessed with three beautiful children, a great marriage, and lived in paradise. Ron, Karyl, Alicia, Carren and Scott.

Above: I loved holding the violin in my hands. It was so delicate and I felt a sense of pride and accomplishment when playing.

Right: Eighth grade confirmation ceremonies administered by Pastor Darold Reiner. Carren stood tall, declaring her Christian values and beliefs.

Left: Carren at age three: I had a great life growing up. I knew my Mom and Dad loved me and just as important they loved each other.

Below: Carren posing with her mighty steed "Mickey." He terrorized Carren's older sister by biting, but was humbled by a mighty blow from Carren's hands.

Carren enjoying life before heading
off to the big kids' school in the fall.

SUWS graduation: After 21 days in the Idaho
wilderness, the girls and staff hike out for a
reunion with family. Mom telling Carren she loves
her even though she is a little smelly.

Carren and Karyl posing in the courtyard at the
Caribbean Center for change. It was our first
official visit and we all agreed: "There is life after
Meth."

Above: Typical girl's laundry day at TB. Karyl verifying everything is clean and asking, "You did these all by hand?"

Left: Family Reunion at Tranquility Bay. As the program puts it, "Making a whole and healthy family."

Left: Scott's graduation from Marine Boot Camp at the Marine Corps Recruit Depot, San Diego. A family in healing.

Below: 5 years of sobriety, life at its best in the "Last Best Place", Yellowstone National Park, Montana and Wyoming.

The next day, lying in bed drifting in and out of sleep, I looked up and there was Carren standing at the doorway of my room. She stood there tall and beautiful, yet horribly thin and pale. There were dark circles under her eyes and there appeared to be sores on her face and arms. She was wearing the same clothes as when I had seen her at Red's a few nights before: black short skirt, white top and black high heels. She was terribly sick and strung out, but she looked so wonderful to me. I thought maybe this was what God had planned. Me going to the hospital would make Carren change her life – maybe she would finally give up meth.

Carren just stood there and looked at me, sullen eyes, with a vast distance between us.

'Carren, could I have a hug'?

She stared at me for a short time, then shook her head no and walked from the room. I wanted to scream for her to come back: *Please, Carren, I am sorry, I love you, come back, please!* Instead, I just heard the click of her high heels as she walked down the hall. I was convinced that I would never see Carren alive again. She was gone – meth had taken another child and this time it was my little girl.

When Karyl came by for the afternoon visit, I related the day's events.

'Carren came by to see me today.'

Karyl's excitement was instant. 'How is she doing? Is she coming home? Ron this is great – when do I get to see her?'

It had been over five months since Karyl had seen Carren and my first thought was that I hoped Karyl never saw Carren looking the way she did that day. I told her every detail of the visit and tears filled Karyl's eyes.

'Is she going to die Ron? Are these drugs going to kill her before we can get her help?'

I didn't answer the question. We held each other in our arms and cried.

The nurse came in several times due to the irregularity of my monitoring equipment but left us alone to deal with what we started to believe was the inevitable death of our daughter.

I was released from the hospital a couple of days later and was given instructions to minimize stress, get lots of rest and try to enjoy life for a change. My doctor cared for our family a great deal and knew our circumstances. She offered whatever help she could, but emphasized that I would be of no help to Carren if I were not alive to help. Karyl and I went home convinced that the next call we received concerning Carren would be from the coroner advising us that she was dead.

Even so, Karyl intensified her efforts to find long-term treatment for Carren once she became available to us. Watching Karyl organize every detail in her now giant – and now almost filled – binder titled 'Saving Carren,' gave me a new sense of love and respect for the woman with whom I had spent the last 32 years of life.

We had withdrawn from most of our friends over the course of the last few months. It was hard to have casual visits and get togethers just for fun, when life wasn't fun any longer. Bob McConnell and friend from the old days (before meth) accused us of cocooning ourselves, pushing friends away. I knew what he was saying was true, but it seemed Karyl and I had done all we could do and it hadn't been enough. Meth had won and all I wanted was to be alone.

I found myself drinking more. One glass of wine at night just to relax, then one in the afternoon before Karyl got home from work. Soon I was drinking wine on every day, all day, yet not feeling any better. I had always joked in days past that I wasn't into quality when drinking, just into quantity. It has always been a joke because alcohol had never been one of my favorite pastimes. Yet here I was tapping the wine box in the refrigerator again and it wasn't 10 o'clock in the morning yet. I was becoming a drunk in less than a week's time and I hated life for being a failure as a dad, and I couldn't depend on my health any longer.

One morning I was sitting on the back deck; It was cold outside and I had just finished the second water glass of my Costco box of Chablis. The world seemed overwhelming and I didn't want to live another day. I kept thinking what the doctor said: just rest and avoid stress. Yeah right, Carren was dead already as far as I knew.

I made the decision I didn't want to live any longer and retrieved my 357 Smith & Wesson revolver from my gun cabinet. I had observed suicides in the past and never saw any of the successful participants express any regret. I thought about it for a while, how to go about it. I didn't want to miss and end up an invalid in some nursing home. I decided the best way was to place the gun in my mouth and pull the trigger.

As I sat there, gun in hand, our dog Hobi started licking my hand.

He just looked at me and licked my hand over and over and nuzzled my knee. Just for a brief second I started thinking about what I was about to do. Just enough pause to make me ask out loud, 'What are you thinking?'

I realized that, once again, I was considering taking the easy way out. What a coward I had become. I still had Scott and Alicia to think about and Karyl. Regardless of my faults, she still loved me. I started to cry and asked God to help me, help save Carren, and my family!

I heard the door close in the garage and Karyl was standing watching me from the window.

'What are you doing?'

'Oh, I was just doing a little target practicing at the stump out in the field.'

'Ron, you know Hobi hates the sound of guns. Go put that thing away and I will make dinner.'

It was almost four o'clock and the entire day had passed and I couldn't remember anything since late morning. I promised myself tomorrow would be different.

I finally forced myself to go back into my office. My business hadn't entered my thoughts over the past few weeks. Staying at home meant continuing to drink and unrelenting depression; going to work meant trying to live again. I decided to try life. As I look back, it seems ironic I was choosing life at the same time Carren was making her choice for death.

CARREN

I left the hospital and never looked back. I realized all the hurt I had caused my family and didn't want to continue the way I was living. I just didn't know how to stop.

When we got back to the house where we were staying I decided I wanted out and told my friends I was going to kill myself. They tried to talk me out of it for a while, but every one of us had considered death as an option one time or another. Finally they agreed to help and said they would throw a goodbye party as soon as we got enough money to buy some shit.

We all sat around and planned the party for next weekend. Before this last party, I had things I wanted to say. I sat down and wrote my parents a note and told them what I wished I had said at the hospital.

Mom and Dad, I am sorry. You have said over and over: 'I don't know how life got so crazy and out of control.' I don't really know myself. There were so many times I didn't have a place to stay and I felt so lost. It didn't start out that way. When I started out using drugs, it was supposed to be fun and also keep me going. Instead it just brought me down. Basically, I just didn't look at the big picture. When it finally got so bad and I was disgusted with my life, I just decided that this is what I deserved. I really believed this was how I was going to live the rest of my life.

Life doesn't seem to matter anymore. The only thing I think about is my next high. I don't get as high as I used to when I first started, but the lows are just as bad. When I can't get a high, I feel like I am going to die. It has got to the point where I don't even care about my druggie friends. If I could take their dope I would. I am sorry, Mom and Dad. I wish I could do things over, differently.

I love you, Carren.

My so-called friends all got together the next weekend for another night of getting high and Carren's goodbye party. We had a stash of drugs we had stolen from cars, stuff we had bought, and plenty of beer and wine. I had made my decision to die tonight. My friends had never seen anyone actually kill themselves and were willing to help anyway they could. The party started and I used anything and everything I could. When I couldn't get up to get more pills or beer, my friends brought it over to me. The last thing I remember is someone asking, 'Is she dead yet', then shaking me.

I woke up the next morning and wondered if I was dead – at least I wished I had died. I hurt all over and was so sick I couldn't even move. I had already thrown up all over myself and the smell was making me even more sick. There were kids lying on the floor all around me, passed out. I finally was able to make it to the bathroom and threw up over and over. I cleaned myself up as best I could and staggered outside the trailer and started walking. I kept thinking I couldn't even kill myself right. God, I wanted to go home. I needed help. I made it to the nearest gas station and decided to call Brad.

'You sound terrible, Carren, are you OK?'

'Brad, I am sick. I need help!'

15. THE ROAD TO RECOVERY

It is awesomely difficult to recognize and to live with the knowledge we cannot change other people, even those we love the most. The seemingly unnatural process of dealing realistically with the addiction of a loved one is called detaching with love. It means doing what we can to help the addicted person and then honestly admitting our limits ... It means let go, let God.

Dr Robert Dupont, The Selfish Brain

We received a call the following Monday morning from Brad, the youth pastor at our church.

'Ron and Karyl, Carren has attempted suicide. She is alive, but not doing well and is asking for help.'

We couldn't believe what we were hearing. She was alive and wanted help?

Brad continued, 'She is very sick and ashamed, she doesn't want to see you, and I don't want to take the chance of her changing her mind. Is there someone that can take her to the treatment other than you and Karyl?'

We had a plan in place and advised Brad that there was a rehabilitation program waiting for her in the event that we could locate Carren. We had also made arrangements with a retired Los Angeles Police Department friend and his wife to have them transport Carren to her treatment program. Their names were Ray and Pam Shorb and they agreed to be available to travel within an hour's notice, day or night.

Ray knew how desperate we were and reaffirmed his commitment to help. 'You call and we can pick her up at whatever location you want – jail, the hospital, the streets, or wherever.'

As it turned out, she wanted help, so we needed to get her safely to her program before she could change her mind or her drug buddies tried to stop her. For Ray, his sole emphasis was to get Carren out of town and out of harm's way as quickly as possible. We planned to have them pick her up at a pre-arranged location and drive to Spokane, Washington. From there they would catch a flight to Boise, Idaho. We had put in place arrangements to have representatives from the SUWS program meet Carren and the Shorb's at the airport. Ray was to call every hour during the trip on the road, or whenever cell phone service was available.

Weeks before, our educational consultant had recommended that we use someone else to transport Carren other than 'her parents.' It was good advice. I don't believe we would have handled the trip emotionally. The first program that Carren would attend was SUWS, located in the high mountain desert of central Idaho. It was a wilderness survival experience for youth that specialized in detoxification, mental and drug evaluations. Their therapist would conduct mental and drug evaluations for Carren and recommend what they believed should happen next.

We arranged the meeting place and called Ray and Pam to let them know the location. It was Hooper's Nursery parking lot. We called the owners of the nursery and they gladly gave us permission to use the lot and agreed to unlock the gate early. They asked if they could see Carren before she left and possibly give her a hug goodbye. I told them we would have to see how it went and explained that Carren didn't even want to see us before she left. When Brad told Carren where the meeting was to take place she seemed relieved. It was out of the way and Carren said she felt safe going there. Everything was ready; we just had to pray that Carren would show up for the morning meeting.

That was the longest day of our lives. We could live with the fact that Carren didn't want to see us. I would have loved to have held her once more before she left. Karyl and I spent a long sleepless night praying and crying, overwhelmed by doubt and fear that Carren wouldn't make the meeting. We had asked Brad to call us and keep us advised of Carren's activities. He said Carren wanted to go say goodbye to her friends, but that she promised to be at the arranged meeting place in the morning. We begged Brad to not let her go. He said the choice was up to Carren and reassured us that he had faith in her that she wanted help and would be there. We thought he was crazy, but we were not in control.

'Let go, Let God' was all I could come up with. I never really knew what that meant until that night.

We reconfirmed that the Shorbs were ready to transport and re-verified the flight reservations in Spokane. We called the school again and they assured us they would be waiting for Carren at the Boise, Idaho airport. We had packed an emergency travel kit containing all the necessities required by the program and had it all prepared for Carren just in case this day ever arrived.

Brad called early the next morning and advised us that Carren was with him and wanted us to be at the morning meeting. She wanted to say goodbye. Karyl and I both started crying; our prayers had been answered. Carren was alive, she wanted to see us and we were going to be able to hold her in our arms and love her once again. Even though all appeared to be going according to plan, I had called my friends at the police force and arranged for officers to be available, at a distance, just in case Carren had a change of heart.

We arrived there early, accompanied by Ray and Pam. In pulled Brad's car and sitting in the front seat next to him was Carren. She was very thin, pale and unkempt. One thing that a person loses when meth takes over their lives is the spark of life in their eyes. Carren's spark of life was gone.

As the car pulled to a stop near us, Brad stepped from the car and walked over and opened Carren's door. She stepped out and appeared hesitant to say or do anything. I spoke up and advised Carren that we had found a program in Idaho that would help her. Carren looked at Ray and Pam as she stepped out of the car and smiled faintly and nodded hello. I quickly explained that Ray and Pam wanted to be with her when she went for treatment. Carren had always respected and trusted Ray and Pam.

She just looked blankly at them and then Karyl stepped forward and asked if she could have a hug. Carren lunged into her arms and started crying.

'I am sorry, Mom, I am sorry.'

Karyl held onto Carren and they cried together. Karyl just kept telling Carren it was OK and that she loved her. They finally stepped apart and Carren looked at me. She just stared for the longest time, searching my eyes, my face, looking for something.

I just whispered, 'I love you,' and she fell into my arms crying: 'Daddy I am sorry, I wanted to hug you in the hospital. I was too dirty. I love you, Dad, please forgive me. I love you. I love you.'

We held each other for not long enough and then it was time for her to go. She thanked Brad for being there for her and gave him a hug. She entered Ray and Pam's car and started her journey to recovery.

Carren arrived in Gooding, Idaho on March 6th, 2001, just five months after her first use of methamphetamines. A complete medical exam was performed; the psychological evaluation would take much longer. She would spend three weeks marching around the high mountain plains of Idaho, leeching her body of meth. We didn't know much about the recovery process and soon learned the meaning of 'one day at a time.'

We received frequent calls from her psychologist about her progress. Carren was heavily addicted to methamphetamines. Her recovery would take a long time. We were advised to find a long-term rehabilitation program that would be available when she completed SUWS. The educational consultant was assigned this responsibility and she started looking immediately. Within a few days we were told that the only program willing to accept Carren that we could afford was Tranquility Bay, Jamaica.

16. LIFE AFTER METH

Success rates for treating Meth vary widely. Outpatient treatment programs have reported 98% of abusers had already relapsed at least once. Other traditional treatment programs (28 day) report 50 to 70% relapse rate within the first 30 days. Parents should not expect a quick fix. 'A few weeks in a detoxification program will dry out a kid but not fix the addiction. You have to change your whole life, and that takes a long time.

Thomas Farah, Second Chances Recovery Program,
Statesboro, Georgia

CARREN

After my failure at suicide I knew I needed help but I couldn't bring myself to call Mom and Dad. They were the last people I wanted to see. Instead I called Brad, our youth pastor; I knew he would listen and help if he could. Brad told me if I was sincere and really wanted help, I should meet him at our church in the morning. He told me my mom and dad had been in contact with him and had a program that could help. They had already arranged to have friends that I trusted, Ray and Pam Shorb, take me to the program. Brad gave me the details about the flight and name of the program.

He said Ray and Pam were going to fly with me to help with the paperwork, check in, and so on.

Brad had arranged to meet Ray and Pam the following morning in the parking lot of my old job at Hooper's Nursery. I agreed to that location because of the many good memories from working there the summer before. I thought maybe I could even say goodbye to a few of my old bosses and friends. I hadn't seen any of them for over six months. Brad was driving and I sat in the front passenger seat, just wondering how my future life would unfold. I was still sick from all the drugs I had taken, and to be honest, scared to death. Brad was making small talk, I was just staring out the window listening; I had nothing to say.

Brad finally pleaded, 'Carren your mom and dad would like to see you before you go.'

'I do not want to see them, Brad.'

'Carren, they love you and would like to at least say goodbye.'

'I don't care, I just want to get out of this town and get this over with.'

The thought of how I had lived over the last few months kept coming to mind. I just couldn't see them. I was so dirty. I had hurt them so terribly and knew they could never forgive me for what I had done to each of them; to my family. In an attempt to change the subject I asked Brad about the treatment program my parents had selected.

'Have you heard about it before?'

Brad just sat there looking forward and said nothing.

I didn't really care if he answered me, I had heard about treatment programs already from my friends. I would spend a month sitting around talking about drugs. There would be some counselor or someone who would supposedly help us learn to live our lives without getting high. I didn't know how that would be possible; I couldn't go a day without getting high or at least thinking about it. I had no idea of how I could ever go a month. Supposedly this program was in Idaho, somewhere out on a ranch and they were good working with kids. I hoped they had horses; maybe I could ride again. But it really didn't matter, all I knew was I wanted to get out of this town, I didn't want to see anyone when I left, and I didn't care if I ever came back. Brad just looked at me, waiting.

I kept mulling over in my mind what Brad had said. After all they are my mom and dad, they were going to pay for my treatment, and maybe I could just see them briefly before I left. Finally without looking at Brad I agreed: OK, they can be there when I go. Let's get this over with.

It was early in the morning and Hooper's wasn't open for business yet. As we crested the hill I could see several cars in the parking lot. Mom and Dad's car was there and another car I didn't recognize. Probably Ray and Pam; I laughed out loud, what am I doing here? Although I said I didn't want to see Mom and Dad, deep inside I actually hoped they would be there. Brad pulled into the parking lot, stopped the car and got out. He walked over to my mom and dad and was introduced to Ray and Pam.

Mom looked really tired. I had not seen her in over three months, and although beautiful, she seemed to have aged several years. Dad looked, I don't know, better than in the hospital but still kind of broken and worn out. I finally got out of the car and Dad began telling me briefly about the program, saying something about the name SUWS.

I stared and then looked over at Mom. She started crying and held out her arms to me. I couldn't believe how much I loved her and missed her. How could I have walked out of my house just three months before without even a hug? I ran to her and fell into her arms. She just held me, both of us crying. She stroked my hair and kept telling me she loved me. I didn't want to let go.

I looked over at Dad and he had tears running down his cheeks. Although tired, there seemed to be a sense of joy I hadn't noticed in the hospital. I stepped back from Mom and looked at Dad. He reached out and took me into his arms. I was crying, he was crying, heck when I opened my eyes, everyone was crying. We were going to be a family again. Suddenly, I realized my old bosses and friends from Hooper's were standing around us. They had tears in their eyes and were smiling.

Eventually I got a hug from everyone there. Ray and Pam finally informed us it was time to go if we were going to catch our flight. I hugged Mom and Dad again and told them I was sorry and that I loved them. They just hugged me again and said they would be here for me when I completed my program. Completed my program, I wondered what that really meant, I had no idea.

I arrived at SUWS the next morning. It was located way out in the middle of nowhere. The first thing I noticed was there were no horses. I was introduced to my counselors, my psychologist, plus six other girls. We were told we would be spending most of our time together. One big happy family, all going through the program together: Each of the girls was from a different town or city and each of us had different problems. The ages ranged from 14 to 18 years old. Our homes were from all over the United States; Texas, California, New York, Montana etc. Most of us had used drugs of one kind or another, and suffered from a wide range of emotional problems but, I was the only meth addict. We were given medical exams, good food to eat and then issued hiking and camping gear. They showed us a bunkhouse where we were going to sleep the first night and were told we would be taking off on a two-week hike into the mountains early in the morning. Mom and Dad never said anything about hiking around the desert for two weeks. I have to admit I started thinking this might not have been such a good idea.

For the first week we marched around the mountains of central Idaho. We slept on the ground, had to make our own food and if we wanted a hot meal we had to learn to start fires with friction sticks. There were two counselors with us at all times. I was the tallest girl in the group and was given the water purification system to carry. With all the stuff we were required to carry, I knew there was no way we would get very far.

The first day was full of complaints from all the girls about sore feet, sore legs, aching backs, too cold, too hot, etc. We made camp early and wanted a hot meal for sure. We each tried to get the fire started but it was no use. Even after the counselors repeatedly showed us, we couldn't get it figured out. We all resigned ourselves to eating dried lentils and water for dinner that evening and based on our latest performance, probably for several nights to come. Regardless of the lack of hot food, I had a full night's sleep for the first time that I could remember. The stars were spectacular, the air was fresh and crisp, and I had a cuddly sleeping bag. I almost forgot about meth for a little while.

I had officially been at SUWS for about a week and a half, and was feeling pretty cocky about my outdoor abilities. I earned the responsibility of starting the fires at night since mastering the bow and spindle friction technique. I prided myself on not having to eat a cold meal since the first night. Being from Montana brought some undeserved credit for knowing about camping and the like. I had been camping with my family on occasion, but to be honest Dad had done most of the work. Anyway, after mastering the fire-making process many of the girls thought of me as the ultimate outdoors person.

We had been on the trail for several hours and it was mid afternoon when we approached our camping location for the night. There was a little creek meandering through large rocks in the valley floor. Not far from the creek's edge the terrain rose abruptly all around us and I thought to myself that this could make things interesting trying to find a flat spot for sleeping tonight. I was just finishing my thought when the counselors informed us that we were not actually camping next to the creek but would be camping at the top of the steep incline that was to the left.

All I could think about was 'We have to climb that? We're here for rehab, not to become mountain goats.'

I didn't take a lot of time to fill my canteens before I mounted my pack and began the intense climb. As soon as I reached the top I sat down, exhausted. We were on this little plateau that overlooked the most incredible desert scenery. It was beautiful and by far the best spot we had camped yet. It was as though we had climbed into a rock fortress and I had this sense of relief and 'being safe.' We were told that we were each to pick a spot to sleep and that we wouldn't be allowed to talk to each other until further notice.

I picked out a spot which seemed to be the best. It was bordering the ridgeline and had a massive rock formation that towered above me. Two of the girls from our group had similar ideas and selected locations on each side of me. The large rock formations towered overhead and actually covered us like a granite ceiling. I began to set up camp which meant collecting the firewood that I knew I would need for a hot meal. I loved a good fire at night. I knew from my dad's lessons during our family camping events that a good fire would keep wild animals at bay as well as provide light, forcing back the darkness.

Everything was set up for the night; my doughnut tarp surrounded my sleeping bag, I had firewood, and water for cooking. All I had to do was sit, think about life, and wait for nightfall. I wasn't fond of the whole silence thing so I decided to break out my journal and record several of my thoughts. At least I could talk to myself via paper and not have people think I was crazy.

Journal entry, p. 100

I am happy to be alive and I look forward with excitement to whatever my future holds. I feel strong about what I am capable of accomplishing. I know I can do whatever I set my mind to. I also recognize my responsibility for my decisions.

Maybe twenty minutes or so had passed and light was fading fast. Suddenly I heard several rocks tumble down the rocky embankment next to me. I looked up immediately to see what was crawling into my campsite. I started screaming, it was the biggest squirrel I had ever seen and it appeared to be after me. All the others girls came running. The female counselor started laughing when she saw me cowering in fear of this creature. It scurried away before she could get control of her laughing and explain that it was a 'rodent of unusual size,' also known as a marmot. I was embarrassed how I had let my imagination get away from me. The other girls got a good laugh as well, but had to admit they had never seen a squirrel, rat or dog as big as that marmot. When we finally settled down and crawled into our sleeping bags the comments started flying. Obviously, the silent campsite left with the marmot.

'Hey Carren, I hope that giant squirrel doesn't come back to eat you.'

'Carren did you know that was just a baby marmot, the mommy and daddy's can weigh up to 100 lbs and are meat-eaters.'

It was all in fun and I really enjoyed the friendships that were developing among the girls and staff.

The psychologist's name was Wendy and she joined us at the campsite most of the evenings after the first few days and would occasionally join us on the trail during the days. None of us girls had any idea how she just showed up the way she did. She just seemed to appear out of the dark as we were sitting around the campsite or would be waiting on the trail as we rounded a bend. We had been hiking for days and were out in the middle of some desolate high mountain desert. How did she know where to find us?

The first week was really hard for me. I was sick most of the time. After the first night, I had trouble sleeping, yet the hikes and fresh air seemed to make each day a little better. I started craving food and couldn't wait for the next meal.

By the second week I started to feel really good. There wasn't a moment I didn't think about getting high, but the cravings only lasted until the next mountain we had to climb. The other girls each had their own problems; each of us had to find our own way to live life again. We spent many more days and nights with the counselors and psychologist and hiked forever through the scenic Idaho terrain. After the second week, we hiked back to a camp and each of us had to spend three days in our own private tent, thinking and writing about our choices that brought us to Idaho. The psychologist spent several hours each day and evening with me, helping me to understand what I had done to myself physically and mentally. I constantly wrote reflections in my journal and occasional letters to Mom and Dad. Graduation was in a few days and I had so much I wanted to thank them for. Most of all I just wanted another chance to hug them and tell them how much I loved them.

After completing the three days in camp, we packed up and headed back out to the wilderness. I looked forward to the physical exercise and the constant beauty of the high desert and mountains; it kept my mind off the cravings for meth. We were making camp when Wendy walked into the campsite. She asked if she could talk to me alone. I enjoyed our talks and eagerly joined her. In the back of my mind I kept wondering how the heck she just showed up out of nowhere. She didn't even look like she was breaking a sweat. We walked away from camp and sat down. Wendy started talking calmly.

'Carren, you are severely addicted to meth.'

'Yeah, I know,' I said, 'that is why I am here. But I am healthy now.' Heck I had already gained about fifteen pounds regardless of how many miles we walked.

She again started to talk. 'Carren, I am recommending that you don't go home. I am planning on telling your parents you need to attend a long-term rehab program for your addiction to meth.'

I instantly replied, 'What another few weeks here or what? Great, I am ready, I love the hikes.'

'No Carren, this program is for initial detox and evaluation. For some kids, things work out and they go home. You have been using meth for over five months.* Your brain has changed, you have changed; your life has changed. It is going to take time to get your life back.'

'Yeah, so what are you talking about?' I asked.

'You will be attending a program for at least six months,' she replied. 'It will be a residential facility somewhere. Your parents are searching for a program now and we will know which one by the time you graduate in a few days.'

I started crying, I couldn't believe I wasn't going home. When I lived on the streets, home was the last place I ever wanted to be.

---

* 85% of meth users become severely addicted with one-time use. It is the most addictive illicit chemical ever released on the streets. One-time use alters the brain structure in the ventral tegmental area programming neurons for future uncontrollable use (Dr Mary F. Holley, *Crystal Meth: They Call it Ice*, 2005).

Now I was sober and it was the only place I could think of. When we walked back to camp, some of the other girls were crying as well. I guess there would be several of us not going home.

It was finally graduation day. I had never graduated from anything in my life – well, maybe kindergarten or confirmation. Anyway, it was the best feeling I have ever experienced. I was going to see Mom and Dad, get to eat real food, and take a long, hot shower. I may be going to a program somewhere, but for now that was the farthest thing from my mind.

We packed up camp at about 6 am and started hiking south, back to the ranch. As we crested a hill we could see cars parked on an old dirt road down below in the valley. There were several people standing around on the road and they seemed to be pointing up at us. After several minutes of hiking in their direction, I finally recognized Mom and Dad. The other girls also began picking out there parents. One of the girls couldn't see her parents. As it turned out, they had been delayed for some reason.

We finally reached the group of parents; Mom, Dad and I hugged each other as if we hadn't seen each other for a lifetime. Mom and Dad looked great. They didn't look as haggard as the day I left for SUWS three weeks ago, give or take a day. We shared stories, our experiences, and hugged each other over and over. We finally headed back to the ranch for graduation, showers, and real food. It was the best day ever and another day without meth.

While we were eating dinner, Mom and Dad explained they had made arrangements for my next program: the Caribbean Center for Change, Tranquility Bay, Jamaica. They knew I liked dolphins, the beach and tropical weather, thus their selection. I asked if they had ever been there. Dad explained he had a mission pastor from our church go visit the facility and he felt it was a good program. I thought, *Jamaica, holy cow!*

The plans were to drive to Salt Lake City, Utah and fly to the Caribbean from there. Dad had scheduled the flights so we had a couple of days to sightsee and visit. Mom was going to take me, Dad wanted to get home to Scott. He was beginning to have behavioral problems at school and wasn't keeping up with his academics Dad admitted. He and Mom hadn't given Scott much attention over the last few months and Scott needed him there. For the first time I thought of my little brother and realized how difficult this must have been for him. What had I done?

'Mom and Dad, how is Alicia doing?'

'OK. She is bitter and angry over life's events. She did tell us to say hi and hoped you are doing better.'

We left SUWS after tearful goodbyes and headed to Salt Lake. It was late and Dad suggested we find a motel with a pool somewhere and finish the rest of the trip tomorrow. Swimming in a pool; that sounded too good to be true. It was nearly 7 pm before we finally found a motel. We talked almost the entire time as we drove through majestic mountains and high desert landscapes. I wanted to know how all of our family was doing. How was Grandma and Grandpa, Nana, my great-grandma.

'Oh and how's your work, Dad. Is Mom still working at the fabric store taking fabric in lieu of pay, building up her fabric stash?'

I wanted to know everything, and yet, it was just as if I hadn't been gone all these months.

As we were checking into the motel Dad spelled out the rules. I was not to make any unauthorized phone calls. He or Mom needed to be present when and if I made a call. Mom or Dad needed to be with me at all times, unless it was in the bathroom. Absolutely no drugs, smoking, or alcohol.

I agreed completely and we started taking our luggage up to the room. We planned on going swimming first and then out to dinner. Dad went down to get some more of our luggage and Mom excused herself to the bathroom. I still can't believe what I did; as soon as Mom went into the bathroom I decided to call my old druggie friends just to say hi and let them know what I had been up to for the last month. I charged the call to our motel room and requested the operator connect me to my so-called friend, my old drug dealer. The phone started ringing immediately.

'Hello?'

'Yea, this is Carren, how are you guys doing?'

'Who is this?'

'It's me Carren, Carren Clem; I have been gone for a while; my Mom and Dad have me in a rehab program.'

Again they asked: 'Who is this?'

'This is Carren, you assholes, don't you remember?'

'No I don't,' and then the phone went dead.

I looked up and there was Dad watching me.

'What did you do, Carren?'

'It's OK, Dad, I just called my old friends to let them know I was clean and everything was OK.'

'Carren, did you mention where you were? Do they have caller ID?'

'It's OK, Dad, believe me. They have caller ID, but they don't even know where Idaho is.'

Dad immediately replied, 'Carren, our family has been repeatedly threatened by your so-called friends. One of your good buddies pulled a gun on me just a few weeks ago. They have been looking for you all over for the last four weeks. You have just jeopardized our lives by giving out the information of where we are staying.'

I started crying and Mom came out of the rest room to ask what was going on.

'Pack up the bags,' said Dad, 'we have to leave immediately. We can't take the chance that Carren's old drug dealers won't come down here, or call someone down this way to come after her.'

Dad was genuinely afraid. I had never seen him like this before. We checked out of the motel and headed straight for Salt Lake. He called a friend of his who worked with the FBI in Salt Lake and got information on a safe hotel where we could stay. I just sat in the back seat and cried the entire way. I finally started to realize what my choices had done to my family. Jamaica started sounding better than ever.

We spent the night in Salt Lake. The motel didn't have a pool and for the most part I was too tired anyway. I apologized to Mom and Dad, over and over.

Dad finally told me, 'Carren, it's OK. We told you we accepted your apology. Let's just move on and enjoy the time we have left before you and Mom leave.'

We had a great morning and arrived at the airport in plenty of time for our afternoon departure. After getting the luggage and ourselves checked in, it was time to say goodbye. Dad gave me a big hug and told me he knew I could be a success and that he loved me. He gave Mom a hug goodbye and we started through security. I stopped and looked at Dad walking away.

'Dad, Dad,' I shouted and ran back to him. I gave him a hug and told him how much I loved him. 'Thank you, Dad, for not giving up on me, I will work my hardest to get well. Dad, will you do me a favor? If there is anyway you can help my friends that are still using, will you try? They won't have a chance if someone doesn't help. Most of them don't have families that care.'

Dad promised he would do something – he didn't know what but would figure it out.

I gave Dad a final hug and joined Mom in the security line. We went through the final gate and started walking toward the plane as I looked back one last time. Dad was gone. I didn't realize it then, but it would be seven months before I would see him again.

Our arrival to Jamaica was bizarre. The airport didn't have a jetway and as soon as the door of the plane opened, the heat and humidity rushed in. We exited the plane and walked to the terminal for processing by customs. Almost everyone was black except the tourists. For the first time I got the sense of what it must be like for racial minorities in the States. I stood out and it seemed every one of the natives was watching Mom and me. We headed out the front doors of the terminal where we were told there would be a taxi waiting to take us to Treasure Beach and my new school. There amongst the hundred or so cabbies was this slight little black guy holding up a sign with the name Clem written in bold print. Mom waved and before we knew it we were loaded and headed off across the island to the south side of Jamaica.

In Jamaica, everyone drives on the wrong side of the road. At home everyone drives on the right side of the roadway and it felt weird to be doing just the opposite. I don't think the Jamaican cars have brakes, and absolutely have overactive accelerators and horns. As we headed through the city of Montego Bay, the engine raced, the horn honked and our driver kept yelling out the window in some language we didn't understand. We started climbing the mountains going out of town and our driver stepped on the accelerator more; the car started speeding up faster and faster. When our driver came upon another car, he would sound his horn, swerve around the obstacle and hit the brakes as he reentered his lane, squeezing in between the other cars.

Just when we thought we could relax and breathe again he would step on the accelerator and off we would go again. Sometimes other cars were driving directly in our direction and he would have to swerve back into his lane to avoid a head-on collision. Mom never swears and she said 'shit' twice. For that to happen I knew our life was in imminent danger. It was a four-hour-long ride from Montego Bay to Treasure Beach. I can say without a doubt that by the time we got there I had a closer relationship with God. Both Mom and I must have prayed for him to save us more times than I can count.

We checked into the school and Mom took a tour while I sat in the courtyard. After her tour we checked into the hotel in Treasure

Beach for our last night together. Unless God made a personal call to Mom, I would start school tomorrow.

The next day Mom and I arrived back at the facility. We unpacked all my gear from the car. Mom gave me a hug goodbye and I was asked to accompany a few of the female students. I didn't see Mom leave. Initially I was scared, angry and to be honest overwhelmed. My mom had just left me alone in a foreign country and now I had people telling me I needed to start working this thing called a 'program'. I was introduced to the group of girls I would be living with and told they would act as my family while in the program. When one of the girls told me she had already been in the program for more than a year and a half, the reality of what lay ahead of me finally hit home. I started to cry and did so for the next three days. What had I done to my life and what hope did I have for a future?

My program started immediately and to be honest for the next seven months I was so busy with school, counselors, psychologist, and trying to put my life back together, I never gave going home much of a thought. Jamaican food took some getting used to but in time I began to enjoy all the aspects of my new home. For the first time I was successful academically in school. I joined a rape crisis group and started dealing with all the pain and hurt from my past choices. There was life after meth and for the first time I began to believe I would be able to succeed.

I knew I would be a drug addict the rest of my life. It was my choice if it would be in recovery or relapse. There *is* life after meth; it just takes a lot of love, determination, and forgiveness. My family gave me plenty of each.

17. A TRIP TOO FAR

Drug treatment and rehabilitation for methamphetamines addiction is complex, long-term, and expensive. Any family participating in a treatment program should conduct in-depth research to determine the success rate for treatment, the extent of psychological care provided, educational opportunities for the person in recovery, the commitment to family training, and what if any after care and family support are provided. Treatment for methamphetamine requires long-term intense in-patient and outpatient therapy, and often the quality of after care is the determining factor for success,

Ron Clem, Teens in Crisis

Neither Karyl nor I had any experience with Jamaica, long-term rehabilitation programs, or residential treatment facilities in general. After consulting with the few meth experts I could find and conducting extensive research, I realized that Carren's treatment could last for up to two years. Meth had altered her brain structure significantly, thus requiring a prolonged behavior modification program to heal and retrain her brain. I was told that meth was different: it had most likely damaged the cells in her brain that produce the neurotransmitter dopamine, and it would take time for her brain to heal. Over time with counseling and separation from drugs and alcohol, Carren could learn to live her life clean and sober.

After calling several other treatment programs in an attempt to learn about meth recovery I learned that most traditional treatment facilities involving meth were short-term, typically 28 days, and had dismal success rates. The thought of Carren spending two years in treatment had substantial financial implications. Carren's lifestyle while living on the streets had created several medical issues for her that would require time and money to heal. The combined costs of her medical and treatment were going to be significant for us and we were advised we needed to start planning for the anticipated $80,000 to $100,000 dollar costs for treatment.

Karyl had been apprehensive about sending Carren out of the country for rehab and the thought of her being gone for two years seemed overwhelming for her. For me, I had located an Aids mission clinic in Nigeria, Africa, associated with our church that was looking for volunteers and I would have sent Carren there had Karyl not found a program that would accept her. I had made up my mind that I would do anything to separate Carren from her meth use: Watching what meth was doing to her here at home in the Flathead Valley overshadowed any concerns I may have had of sending her to a foreign country.

Just the same, I knew that to quell Karyl's fears I would need to investigate the Caribbean Center for Change and verify that it was safe and had the necessary care Carren needed. After checking with the State Department office in Kingston, Jamaica and the mission Pastor working in Kingston, affiliated with our church, Karyl and I came to the conclusion that Carren would spend the next year or so trying to recover her life in St Elizabeth Parish, Tranquility Bay, Jamaica.

With all the decisions made relating to Carren's future treatment in place, we were ready to attend her graduation from SUWS. The psychologist from SUWS had advised us that Carren held on to extreme guilt due to her last five months on the streets in the Flathead Valley. She expressed concerns that her mom and dad would not be able to forgive her for the things she had done: for what she had become. Regardless of what we wrote in our letters: how much we loved her, how important she was in our lives and that whatever happened in the past would stay in the past, Carren was still afraid and full of shame. We were advised to prepare ourselves for a difficult meeting and that her success in the next program would/could be affected if she wasn't convinced of our love and commitment to her. Karyl and I both knew that if we could just hold her in our arms again, if we could just tell her how much we loved and cherished her, she would know there was nothing left to forgive.

We drove all night to get to Gooding, Idaho for Carren's graduation. Upon arrival at the facility we were advised that the kids were coming in from the mountains and we could walk up the road to greet them. There had been seven other girls in Carren's group: six of the girls had parents present. One of the girls' parents had called and informed the staff that they were still vacationing and wouldn't be able to attend their daughter's graduation. That was difficult to understand and I almost caught myself thinking: no wonder their daughter was in a program. Then I wondered what had I done to cause my daughter to be here. I decided to keep the famous adage 'Judge not other parents lest we be judged' as one of the foundations of our family's recovery!

After walking down the road about a quarter of a mile, we could see a single line of hikers coming down a mountain trail. I couldn't tell who was who. They all had on similar clothing, backpacks, stocking caps and big smiles on their faces. The groups of parents were nervous and questions were passed from Mom to Dad and vice-versa – can you see her? Which one is she? Before long we could each make out our daughters. They all had dirty faces, bright eyes, and beaming smiles.

As they came up the trail toward us, Karyl and I held each other, tears in our eyes, not believing how good Carren looked. After seeing how good she looked we knew we were going to get our daughter back. After hugs, tears and more hugs, the counselor said there is one thing that we as a group needed to do before heading to the ranch houses for showers and meals. Each of the girls had taken two pieces of paper and placed one word, of great personal meaning for them, on each piece of paper. The papers had been mixed up and we each reached into a hat and selected one.

The instructions were simple; we were to read out loud the word on the paper and share the significance it had for us personally. The first mom read hers: 'forgiveness'. She replied, 'I ask for forgiveness for all of our family so that we can have love in our home again.'

Then her husband read his paper: 'anger'. 'I want the fear of losing my daughter to go away so that I can quit being angry with my wife, my daughter, and myself.'

And so it went until it was my turn. I opened the piece of paper: 'love'. Tears came to my eyes and I couldn't stop crying.

Carren came over to me and hugged me and said, 'It's OK, Dad, I love you.'

I replied: 'I'm sorry I wasn't there for you, that I couldn't protect you. I love you Carren.'

Carren hugged me and we both cried and she said softly, 'I am going to make it, Dad. Thank you for not giving up on me.' It was a great day!

Our next decision was who would take Carren to Jamaica. We finally agreed that Karyl would take Carren, and I would head home to be with Scott. He had been left alone long enough and he needed one of us home now. Scott was beginning to withdraw from our family and was spending more time away from home. As a family, we had not been there for him when he needed us, resulting in him searching elsewhere for love and attention. Counselors at his school had recently advised us of concerns due to the new friends he was associating with. After much discussion between Karyl, Carren, and I all agreed he needed his dad.

Karyl and Carren's flights for Jamaica departed from Salt Lake City, Utah. Our trip from SUWS to Salt Lake was filled with reflections of our lives before Meth. None of us wanted to remember the horrors of the last five months. We all had great hopes of returning to the lives we shared before the rape and drug abuse. Often Carren would start crying and just whisper she was sorry. All we could do as parents was hold her and love her with everything we possessed inside.

Carren's psychologist's final words were simple: 'There are no guarantees. Believe me; you are in for a long struggle – all of you. Love one another unconditionally and remember: you have been given a second chance – make the most of it.'

We arrived at the airport with little time to waste. After we checked in and the flights and gates were confirmed, it was time to say goodbye again. Karyl was apprehensive about traveling alone in a foreign country for the first time. Carren was crying and repeatedly asking if there was another way.

'Are you sure, Daddy, that this is what God wants you to do, us to do?'

I wasn't sure of anything, but I knew that I didn't want Carren returning to the Flathead until the treatment counselors, psychologists, and doctors said she was ready.

'Carren, I love you, you can do this. You are a special girl – my lovely daughter, we love you and will be here for you, I promise! Karyl, you can do this. If you sense anything isn't right, you and Carren get on a plane and head home, I love you.'

They were just preparing to enter the departure gates when Carren turned and ran back to me and gave me a big hug. She was crying, 'Daddy, I love you. Daddy, if you can help, there are so many other girls out there just like me. Can you do something to help them? Please, Daddy, they won't live much longer if they don't get help.'

'I will do everything I can, baby girl. I love you. Work hard so you can come home soon.' She turned and walked away. I had no idea that it would take another year and a half before she would be ready to reenter the real world or live at home again.

Their flight left without incident and I started the long drive home from Salt Lake to Kalispell. The uncertain future, the impact of events over the last five months, and the sense of relief that Carren would at least have a chance at life after meth, finally hit me during the nine and a half hour drive home. There were times when I would just stop and cry uncontrollably. At other times I found myself smiling to myself, thankful that we finally had a chance to put our family back together.

Carren's treatment and recovery at the Caribbean Center for Change, Tranquility Bay, Jamaica would be the greatest challenge in her life. Even though she had detoxed significantly at her first treatment program at SUWS, the depression, guilt and despair associated with the recovery from meth soon became a part of her life. She was assigned a family of girls. Their group name was Foundation Family. Her schedule was busy: A typical day was as follows: wake up at 6:30 am, get dressed, room inspection, break-fast at 7:30, personal counseling and psychotherapy, 3 hours of school classes, lunch, counseling session, play and exercise time, 3 hours of school classes, group session, dinner, private time for writing, study reflections, and then bed. Regardless of the intense schedule, Carren was struggling with her choices over the last five months while living on the streets.

Some of my most prized possessions are the letters Carren penned during the early days of treatment.

Dear Mom and Dad,
    It is not everyone who gets a second chance at life! I have thought a lot about it. I can't believe how I took a wonderful

life that God gave me and threw it all away. Treating a precious gift like it didn't matter. I remember the weekend I went to Brad for help. I had been out the whole weekend and everything was starting to catch up to me. I was messing up my job. I had lost you guys, Scott and Alicia. As well as everyone else that ever meant anything to me. It seemed the more money I spent on drugs the more it took. Regardless of the amount of drugs I took, it was never enough. I still didn't have the energy to make it through each day. It was horrible waking up in the morning and not knowing what I had done the night before. I had traded a wonderful life with you guys for a life as a dirtbag. It got to the point where I didn't want to take anymore. I felt that I had lost everything and I just wanted to end my life. I got your letter yesterday and it brings tears to my eyes hearing about your friend's daughter, Angie. The weekend before I left for SUWS I was almost one of those daughters. I almost lost God's gift to me of my family: A family that I loved and knew that loved me. For what? I hated life and decided to take my own life. I took every kind of drug I could, while my so-called friends watched. I just didn't care. I gave up all hope. The next morning I woke up and was really sick. I know that I should have been dead, but something happened. I can't explain it except that a miracle happened.

I know that I was in over my head and I know that I am alive today because God has a plan for me. It still amazes me how some people have to be slapped in the face with the truth before they realize what is going on around them. I cannot thank you enough for loving me, supporting me and providing me the chance to get my life back on track.

I love you Mom and Dad.

Carren continued to struggle for many months with the guilt of her choices and the continuing consequences affecting her health and emotional well-being. With each day she appreciated life a little more. Each day the sun was a little brighter. Recovery was beginning, life after meth was becoming a reality.

18. THE MAKING OF A WHOLE AND HEALTHY FAMILY

The family. We were a strange little band of characters trudging through life sharing diseases and toothpaste, coveting one another's desserts, hiding shampoo, borrowing money, locking each other out of our rooms, inflicting pain and kissing to heal it in the same instant, loving, laughing, defending, and trying to figure out the common thread that bound us all together.

Erma Bombeck

One obstacle we knew required immediate attention was that Carren would turn eighteen in four months. That meant she could walk away from treatment regardless of her state of mind or progress in battling her addiction. From all we had been told, Carren's rehab would be a minimum of twelve months, maybe longer. I had heard of an obscure Montana law that allowed extended parental guardianship over an endangered child. In extreme cases, parents were granted control of their children after the age of 18 if it could be proved that the children were incapable of caring for themselves. For God's sake, if anyone should qualify, it should be us.

I made a quick note to call our attorney as soon as I arrived back home to start the process, if in fact such a law existed. He asked if I had any supporting information detailing Carren's drug addiction and current state of mind. I agreed to forward a letter prepared by Carren's treating psychiatrist explaining his findings. I briefly detailed the letter:

I have been acquainted with the Clem family since 1997 and worked specifically with Carren in the spring of 2000. Initially, her working diagnosis was a Depressive Disorder, but issues of alcohol and marijuana abuse were part of the presenting picture. She did well in treatment, but unfortunately, relapsed into severe methamphetamine abuse. This drug addiction escalated swiftly and severely, impacting every area of her life, according to friends and family. In my professional opinion, she was and remains incapacitated and at serious risk for loss of life due to the seriousness and danger of her significant methamphetamine dependence outside of a qualified treatment facility. (Report provided to the court by Carren's psychiatrist)

Our attorney had not been aware of Carren's drug abuse and the impact on our family. He expressed his sympathy and advised us he would prepare the documents for emergency extended guardianship and begin the process for the eventual court hearing. Emergency extended guardianship was granted by the courts; we could rest knowing Carren would remain in treatment for at least six months. The court did require we secure an independent witness to meet with Carren on a weekly basis and provide the court with monthly reports on her progress and condition.

We had previously been in contact with a pastor associated with our church who has a congregation in Kingston, Jamaica. I called and asked him if he had any suggestions. Being aware of our situation he suggested a private psychiatrist living in Kingston. He knew the man personally and advised us that his visits could be utilized as additional psychological treatment for Carren. We submitted the recommendation to the court and Dr Brighten was hired as the site visitation officer for the court. The next problem we faced was how we were going to pay the anticipated cost of Carren's treatment. The residential cost alone was $2500 a month. That didn't include required travel, medical, psychological counseling, the court appointed psychiatrist, incidentals, and any unexpected miscellaneous costs.

Karyl and I agreed we would sell our home to finance Carren's treatment that we now expected to exceed $80,000. We had regrets at leaving the little ranch where we had raised our children and which had so many memories for us. However, we knew that going into debt we could never repay would put undue pressure on our entire family. We needed to plan on life after meth, when Carren would come home. That was when all of our efforts would be needed to save our family. Personal possessions didn't seem to have much meaning any longer.

I arrived home and picked Scott up from our friend's home where he had been staying. Scott's first question: 'How is Carren? When will she be home? Is she going to be OK?'

I replied, 'Scott, Carren is very sick and will need to be in treatment for a long time. When the time is right, we will all go to Jamaica and be a family again.'

Karyl called home, during their transit to Jamaica, whenever there was an opportunity. Carren seemed fine, the flights had been OK and they would fly out in the morning for Jamaica. She agreed to call as soon as they reached Montego Bay and then again when they reached the Caribbean Center for Change, Tranquility Bay. Scott wanted to talk to Mom and Carren and it was one of the best days of my life to listen to him and his sister share experiences and expectations for the future. Before giving me back the phone, he told her how much he loved her and encouraged her to work hard so she could be home soon. We were a family in healing and for the first time I felt that we were going to make it.

I called Alicia in Bozeman and updated her on the previous day's events. She was angry with her sister for the choices she had made and didn't want to talk to Mom or Carren. I tried to explain to Alicia that although it was poor choices on Carren's part about using drugs, there was more to it than that.

'That's all you and Mom ever do is cover and make excuses for her,' she burst out in an angry reply. 'What about the rest of the family? I am in school trying to make something of myself. Are you going to be there for me?'

We had made Alicia a promise when she moved to Bozeman to go to school: if she applied herself and maintained a B plus average, we would help her with her education. I realized what Alicia already knew: we couldn't afford to pay for Carren's rehab and

Alicia's education at the same time. We knew we had to help Carren; for Alicia it was just another promise broken.

Karyl was planning to leave Carren at Tranquility Bay in the morning. She was concerned about what to do if she didn't think the program was appropriate for Carren.

'Karyl, if you don't feel it's the right place, bring Carren home.'

'Ron, this is going to be the hardest thing I have ever done in my life. I am going to make the choice to leave our daughter in a foreign country. Everyone is black here. It is a third world country and they don't know how to drive. Are you sure this is what we should do?'

'Karyl, this is your decision. You do what you think is best, but remember where Carren is coming from. Make the decision for her well-being, not because you want to make it easy on yourself.'

'I love you, Karyl, and I know you will do what is in our family's best interest, in Carren's best interest.'

As soon as I got off the phone, I called our friends and asked if they would call Karyl in Jamaica and give her words of encouragement. That old saying kept coming to mind, 'It takes an entire village to raise a child.'

Karyl toured the facility the next morning and made the agonizing decision to leave Carren. She cried the entire trip back, with brief interruptions of sheer terror due to the harrowing car ride over the mountain pass back to Montego Bay. Carren was in treatment and Karyl was on her way home.

Carren's treatment required her to participate in rape support groups; psychological counseling and a one-on-one weekly visit with a psychiatrist we hired from Kingston, Jamaica. We received weekly updates from her group counselor and psychiatrist. Carren was still in psychological withdrawals from meth, but was beginning to make progress. She had to earn the privilege to talk to us, which would take about three months. But we wrote letters to each other constantly; each of us was making great efforts to reunite our family.

In July 2001, we sent Carren the papers to sign agreeing to extend our guardianship for her until she was 21 or upon graduating the rehab program. We were allowed to talk to her and explain our intentions for the guardianship: encouragement to complete the program, continued medical insurance, assistance with her education after she graduated, and financial support via room and board during her educational pursuits. It was a tough decision, but she agreed that she wasn't ready to take control of her life: She signed the required court documents. The extended guardianship insured that she would not leave the program until completion: she later told us that she probably would have left many times if she hadn't been forced to stay.

In early September, we were advised that family day at Tranquility Bay would be held the first week of October and we should make plans for coming back to Jamaica. Karyl and I would make the first trip and depending on Carren's progress, the entire family would return three months later. We were in Seattle completing a parent-training seminar for Carren's program when the news of the attacks on New York City flashed across the televisions. The horror of the planes hitting the World Trade Center sickened and frightened all of us. Karyl and I were far from home and could only think of getting home to Scott, calling Alicia and somehow reaching Carren's facility. We were concerned for Carren's safety and wondered if we still could get to Jamaica for our family visit. After several calls we learned that Scott was upset with the news from New York, but was OK. Alicia was shaken, but said she was with friends and would be fine. We couldn't reach Carren's facility by phone and decided to head home immediately.

Entering the streets of Seattle the morning of 9/11 was surreal. People in adjacent cars were crying. Everyone was frightened, yet seemed resolved to keep it all together and put extra effort in helping each other. All commercial flights had been cancelled and the highways were crowded with Americans just trying to get home. While driving home we stopped to get gas near a little town called Moses Lake. There were carloads of business travelers who had rented cars to get home and were stopped, attempting to fill up as well. There was a sense of panic when many of the homeward-bound travelers discovered that their credit cards couldn't be validated for some reason. It turned out East Coast phone lines were jammed, preventing verification of credit card purchases. Those of us who had cards that worked filled tanks of displaced travelers and provided cash and assistance however we could. Names, hugs, and addresses were shared amidst tears and an overwhelming sense of patriotism. I was proud to be an American.

After finally arriving home we received a phone call that all the students at Tranquility Bay were fine and that each would call home as soon as possible. Jamaicans felt the pain Americans were suffering; we all knew that the world had changed. We were advised that Family Week was still on and that there were no concerns for the safety of the students at the school.

Karyl and I participated in 'family weekend' in October. It was one of the most emotional weekends of our lives.

We got to hug our healthy and beautiful daughter for the first time in seven months. Carren continually thanked us for saving her life. She admitted that trying to put her life back together after meth was the most difficult thing she had ever experienced. She was happy to be clean and sober and was looking forward to our family reunion in January. After leaving Jamaica our next effort would be coordinating our return visit but this time with Alicia and Scott: a family reunion.

19. TREATMENT: LIFE IN JAMAICA

A community that understands methamphetamine and the nature of addiction will be equipped to fight this scourge with intelligence and compassion. We don't have to stand by helplessly while our children march off the edge of a cliff and our society is brought to its knees by a drug. Crystal Meth – they call it ice.

Mary F. Holley, MD

CARREN

Mom and I finally arrived at the hotel on the south shore of Jamaica. The signs identified the area as Treasure Beach, St Elizabeth Parish, but it was dark and without street lights, there was little hope of seeing what the area was like. In any event I was just happy to have the ride over. I was thinking that if the drive from Montego Bay to Treasure Beach was an indicator of how the rest of my recovery was going to go, I was in for a real tough time. Our hotel was right on the beach and I could hear the waves lapping at the shore from our room. From the window you could see the lights of distant ships, uncountable stars that you could almost touch and feel the gentle ocean breeze blowing through our room. So far, other than Mr Toad's wild ride and being called 'whiteys' by the

Jamaicans, this wasn't too bad. Still, knowing that I was in another part of the world was frightening. After checking into the hotel and freshening up a bit, we went over to my future new school to look things over.

We were given a brief tour of the facility and I can absolutely assure you the school was definitely not what I had been expecting. It was dark so I couldn't see much, but what I did see convinced me I wanted to go home. The school had bars around it and looked like a fortress. I had imagined a kind of resort where I would spend my time blended between the pool, school, and ocean activities. This place looked like it was set up for work, not vacation.

After the tour we went back to the hotel for dinner. As we ate dinner I tried to think of how I was going to keep Mom from leaving Jamaica without me. I pleaded with her to reconsider putting me in this school – so far nothing had worked. Finally, I asked her to call Dad and verify that they were in agreement that this was best for me. As Mom and Dad talked on the phone, Mom cried like I had never seen before. It was breaking her heart to make this decision to leave her little girl behind. My plan was working. She pleaded with Dad to tell her what to do, but Dad kept repeating it was up to her. I almost regretted what I was doing to Mom, but decided getting Mom to change her mind was my only hope at coming home. I felt I had already completed one program; I didn't need to do another one.

After several more phone calls, I thought that for sure I would be heading back to Montana in the morning. It wasn't that I didn't want to change and make my life better; it was that I didn't want to do it here. I didn't care about dolphins and the ocean any more. I was terrified and wanted to go home. Suddenly out of nowhere a woman approached the table and began talking to Mom. I just looked at her and glared. *What did she want?* I thought. She began telling Mom how it would be OK. That this may be one of the hardest decisions ever but at least she will sleep at night knowing her daughter was in a safe place. On and on she went. She told Mom that she had a daughter in the program and it was the best choice she had ever made. I remember thinking: who is this woman? Before long Mom quit crying and appeared to have made her choice. I was going to stay in Jamaica.

After dinner we went back to our room and Mom suggested we take a walk. I saw this as my last chance to get Mom to rethink her decision about leaving me. If I could make her realize I was her special little girl again she would forget all the things that the woman said during dinner. We walked along the beach and Mom talked to me like never before. About her childhood, her marriage with Dad, how frightened she had been when I was on the streets and her fear of never seeing me again. That short little walk gave me a new view of my mom and how special she is. It's kind of funny; we never talked about me coming home.

When it was time for bed I found myself unable to sleep. I still hated the dark and especially here, another strange room. I couldn't get past the feeling that tomorrow I was not going home. Well, by God if I couldn't sleep, neither would Mom. I woke her up and told her to get out her Bible and we could pray some more. Finally exhausted, she said tomorrow we'll just check out the school and if we didn't like it then we can go home. I took that as: tomorrow we are both getting on that plane to the Flathead Valley.

The man came early to pick us up from the hotel. The sun was up and however hard I tried to hate Jamaica, it was no use. The ocean was magnificent, the Jamaican people were unbelievably friendly, and the landscape breathtaking. I was on a beautiful Caribbean island; there were flowers and gardens like I had never seen before. I was in paradise. The trip to Tranquility Bay was much shorter than I had remembered.

In no time at all we where at the front gates. As we got out of the van, we were escorted to the office. There were girls everywhere. The standard uniform was blue shorts with white shirts and flip flops. Most of the girls wearing the uniforms wore their hair tightly restrained. Groups of girls lined up as if they were going to have an inspection or something; they were all standing in straight lines, eyes forward, and silent as if waiting for some special signal or alert.

As we approached the office door two girls came out. They appeared to be my age and they were wearing regular street clothes. One of the Jamaican staff introduced the girls to Mom and me and asked Mom if she had any questions or wanted to look around. I was told rather curtly to stay in the office. As they walked away my mom then began asking questions. It felt like forever before they returned. This time there were two other women with them. They were apparently staff because they had on these light blue shirts and dark blue skirt uniforms with radios strapped to their waists. My mom looked at me and began crying again. She was saying things like 'I love you and I know that this will be a good place for you, just try it for three months.'

It all turned to blur. My fear turned to sheer terror. She was actually going to do it. She was going to leave me here with all these strange people. My fear turned to anger and I lashed out, 'How can you do this to me? Don't touch me, don't ever touch me. You don't know these people. You are going to abandon me again. Well fine, go!'

The rest of the day at Tranquility Bay convinced me Mom really had made a mistake. After checking in at the office, I was given a complete physical by the medical staff. Then two black women escorted me outside into the processing room. Laid out in front of me were all my personal possessions that I had brought with me from the States. It wasn't much because I had just come from SUWS and God knows they didn't let us have much out in the Idaho desert. There were three chairs and one of the staff motioned for me to sit, which I did promptly. They began to go through all my things and instructed me to write my name on them, in specific locations, with a permanent marker.

Suddenly the reality of being all alone in a foreign country and the uncertainty of my future came crashing in. I could feel the tears welling up in my eyes and I started to cry. I know I shared this once before but I was not used to being around blacks, or any minority as far as that was concerned. Montana just didn't have a lot of ethnic diversity. I don't believe I had any preconceived ideas about one race or another, it just made me feel all uneasy and for the first time I realized what it was like to be a minority: it was freaky. The black mamas – wardens, or whatever they were called – attempted to console me, telling me if I worked hard at my program I would be able to go home in no time. Program, what the hell is a program and what did they mean by 'work hard'? I wondered if Mom knew they made you do forced labor at this place.

I felt hopeless. How was I going to follow all the rules? What I wanted now, more than anything, was a hit of meth. I cried off and on most of the first day; my thoughts kept taking me back to my first high, how good it felt and the feeling of invincibility. I promised myself I would never forgive my mom and dad for sending me to this place. For now, I just had to wait and see what the new day would bring.

There were both girls and boys at Tranquility Bay. Each lived in separate areas of the facility and the uniforms were distinctly different. The boy's uniforms were all tan and they all looked like UPS drivers. I was issued the standard uniform for girls: two white short-sleeve blouses, two pairs of blue knee-length shorts and flip-flops. My mom had packed all the undergarments I would need as well as toiletries, special bedding, and of course my Bible. I wanted to know what they were going to do with my new tennis shoes. They told me I had to earn the privilege to wear shoes. Earn to wear shoes? There was no doubt, by that statement, that I was in big trouble.

The next few weeks were a blur. I was assigned a buddy (a senior student) who would be shadowing me for three days. Her name was Tember. She was nice but she scared me a little. She seemed to know all the rules and took them seriously. Tember's job was to acquaint me with the surroundings and help me phase into the daily routine. She walked me around the facility, showing me classrooms, the dining hall, tennis courts, basketball courts and soccer fields. There were a lot of girls and boys at the school, but everything seemed to be operating in a highly organized fashion.

In the afternoon I was introduced to the shower facilities. The girls' showers were located outside in a separate private area adjacent to the girl's dorms.

'What about when it gets cold?' I asked.

One of my escorts replied, 'Hello. You are in Jamaica, a stone's throw from the equator.'

What was I thinking? After finishing with my shower I was introduced to my new family. They were called Foundation. I immediately thought I didn't need a new family I already had one, even though they had abandoned me in some foreign country. There were 14 other girls all from various locations throughout the United States and Mexico. There were blacks, whites, Asians, and Hispanics making up my new family and it was somewhat comforting to realize that color didn't seem to matter as far as getting into trouble went. Each of the girls introduced themselves and my first thoughts were how confident they all seemed. I was older than most of them, yet most were outgoing and appeared to enjoy talking and sharing. Each girl had there own story on why they were at the school. Runaways, suicide attempts, drug and alcohol abuse, criminal behavior, and some were just out of control. One of the girls who had been in the program the longest put it simply: we each earned our way here in our own different way.

We had three women staff assigned to our family for each shift. The girls called them mamas when talking about them, but we were supposed to address them by name: Mrs Meyers or Miss Smith, or whatever. Our lead counselor was named Ms Freeman and each of the girls had tremendous respect and, without a doubt, a certain amount of fear of this woman. I immediately conjured up images of this big black momma, with giant arms and scowling face. I was told I would get my chance to meet her on Monday after lunch during group session. Group session? I didn't have any idea what that meant but soon learned I wouldn't get to participate anyway. I was immediately placed on silence after lunch. I was told it was a process to help me focus my attention on me and why I was here. I could talk to staff and other counselors, but I was not to talk to the girls in my family until given permission.

I had been given all the rules for the facility and to be honest it was overwhelming. I started counting all the rules; there were hundreds of rules to be followed. After counting each of the rules over the course of two days, I had this revelation: I was more like my dad than I realized; counting all the rules is something he typically would do. I started laughing out loud when this thought hit me. The girls in my family all looked at me and must have thought my drug use made me a little goofy. I was on silence and couldn't explain to them what I thought was so funny. As I sat there smiling to myself I thought how weird – being like Dad kind of appealed to me. One minute I hated my parents for leaving me here and the next minute I wanted to be just like them.

I knew there would be no way for me to remember each of the rules, let alone obey them. I was glad I had been given permission to talk to my buddy, because questions constantly kept coming up.

'Why can't we look at the boys? They are right there walking by all the time.'

She explained that if you do you will get a consequence.

'What's a consequence?' I asked.

'You will either lose points, privileges, have to write a 5000 word essay, or be isolated from the other students.'

'Yeah, but how will they know?'

'They just know, believe me. Anyway, you won't have time for boys in this place.'

'When do we get to go to the beach?'

'You don't until you earn the privilege.'

'Well, at least I can look at it, right?'

'No, you have to earn the privilege.'

'OK, Tember, what can I do?'

She was from the upper levels and was scheduled to graduate soon and I could tell she was getting a little frustrated with my attitude. She replied, 'You can go to school, you can take care of your clothes, personal effects, you can make friends, you can eat great Jamaican food, you can get counseling and medical care, but most important; you can get healthy.'

She was younger than I and yet she was talking to me like I was her kid sister. Surprisingly, I appreciated her honesty. She knew everything about Tranquility Bay, yet she wasn't arrogant and didn't look down on me. Everything was just matter of fact and she constantly kept telling me I could do this.

Not only were there rules, but consequences were dolled out when violations were observed. The entire program was based on a points system. You received points when you progressed with your program and lost points when you violated rules, failed to participate in group, were disrespectful, or if you just had a bad attitude. I didn't know how much this was costing my parents, but from the look of things it must have been considerable. I wondered if they knew I had complete control of how long I was going to be here based on my willingness to participate.

Let's see, 267 plus rules, bad attitude, participation, disrespect . . . This was going to cost Mom and Dad a lot.

After a couple of days of adjusting to my new living quarters, I was told it was laundry day. My buddy explained laundry day actually was every other day. I immediately thought with the limited number of uniforms they issued me and the constant heat, every other day may not be enough. I had seen the clotheslines near the showers but no one had told me where the laundry rooms were located. I asked my buddy where the washing machines were and the rest of the family of girls looked at me and started laughing. We all gathered our clothes and the staff escorted us to the courtyard next to our dorm. I was issued a scrub brush, a washtub, soap, and led to the water source.

The staff simply explained, 'In Jamaica missy, we don't have washing machines, you wash by hand.'

I replied, 'You have got to be kidding. This is Dark Ages stuff.' I looked at the other girls and they just smiled and started washing their clothes. 'You mean you just bend down on your knees and start scrubbing?'

One of the girls laughed and replied, 'Welcome to the program.'

The first time it took me almost an hour and a half to get everything scrubbed, rinsed and eventually hung up to dry. One of the girls leaned over and whispered, 'If you get to the point where you get your clothes to squeak when you are rinsing, you have mastered the exercise.'

I knew Mom and Dad wouldn't have approved of this type of treatment – well, Mom anyway. I kept remembering that my mom had said give it three months. In three months I would be eighteen, an adult; then no one could keep me in this place. I decided that I would keep out of trouble and do what I was supposed to. Three months would be no problem and then freedom.

The first letter home I advised them of what I had to endure. Within a couple of weeks I received a letter from Dad and Mom:

Dear Carren
    It is great to hear from you and we are excited to hear how you are enjoying the experience and opportunities of other cultures. When you graduate the program we are looking forward to you showing us how to wash our clothes in a similar manner.

There was other stuff in the letter but I realized sympathy was not included. They made it clear, they wanted me to wash my clothes just like everyone else, but more importantly they were expecting me to graduate this program. What about the deal about giving it three months?

The first couple of weeks went by really fast. I was so busy learning the new routine, adjusting to my 'new family,' testing for school, signing up for and attending school classes, and all the psychological stuff, I had little time to think about using drugs. I followed the rules and was content on biding my time. I had been in Jamaica for about a month when my parents sent me a commitment letter advising me it was their intention for me to graduate the program, regardless of how much time it took. I remember laughing when reading the words 'graduate the program.' Yeah, right, some of these kids had been here for over a year. There was no way that I was going to spend a year in this place. When I turned eighteen years old, I was out of here.

I had group later that afternoon and I was going to share my dissatisfaction over my parents' expectations. I was upset and I knew the girls in my family would agree. My parents had lied to me about how long I would be in the program and I wanted everyone to know.

Group meetings are a little different; you raise your hand and ask permission to speak. When acknowledged, you stand and tell what is bothering you; like you crave drugs, you are upset with your parents, or feel lonely, or whatever. The group was run by Ms Freeman and more often than not she had many of the girls crying when she would ask them to look at there behaviors and choices that earned their privilege to be at Tranquility Bay.

Well, when I shared I knew it would be different. My parents had lied to me and I felt everyone should know how unfair I felt this was. After all, I deserved another chance. I had forgiven my parents and given them a second chance when I had called and asked for help and agreed to meet with them before I left for SUWS. The response was not what I had been hoping for. I was informed that my parents were the ones who had given me a second chance at life and how selfish I was for not appreciating that gift.

One by one all the girls in my family agreed. Ms Freeman then went on to elaborate on my past life and my poor choices. I was standing there crying and she finally asked me, 'Why do you hate yourself, Carren? Don't you think you deserve to have a decent life?'

No one had ever spoken to me like that. Didn't she know I had been raped, not once, but twice (the second time at a party by the druggie Skids). It wasn't my fault I screamed!

'No, Carren, it wasn't your fault, but you cannot continue to live your life based on your rape. That was then and this is now. What are you going to do with your life from here on?'

I stood there crying, suddenly wishing my mom and dad were there to just hold me. At that moment I realized how much I had given up by my drug use, by making poor choices. There was no doubt I needed to be in a program and I did have a lot of work to do. I wasn't ready to go home.

I fell into the routine and began to adjust to my 'new' lifestyle. For the first time in months I was eating three meals a day and was able to sleep in the same bed every night. I began sleeping through the night, although my dreams of the life I was attempting to leave behind often haunted me. I began to take personal interest in the staff and I found that I liked them. They were actually kind people who cared about all of us so-called 'entitled bratty Americans kids.'

I often wondered how these people who could never afford what we considered garbage or cast-offs in America could care about us even though we obviously didn't care for ourselves.

My new family of girls did everything together. Each day we attended school, played sports and games for a physical education class, had group sessions, and so on. Every minute of every day was planned out for us. Life was basic and ultimately easy. My three months were almost over; I had been corresponding with my parents off and on and I felt fairly confident that I would be going home soon, regardless of their constant references to graduating the program. I suppose I viewed my time at Tranquility Bay as some sort of working vacation and would soon be going home.

My parents seemed to take a real interest in the program and all of its little quirks. They were attending all of the same seminars that I was, only at a much faster pace. Typical Dad, I could see him planning each training seminar and projecting the completion date to the exact minute. It infuriated me that they were so active in something in my life and I didn't understand why. All they wanted to do was talk about things they were learning; asking what was I learning and how did I do in my seminars.

Soon other girls in the facility were saying that their parents were talking to my parents and they were all doing seminars together. Not only were they talking, they were comparing information they received from us kids in the program. Often we would make up complaints to see if it would get our parents upset. We would plan it out among us girls and decide who would be the one to start the drama. I told the girls how my mom was anal about fresh food and having food prepared just the right way. One of the girls told her parents how the food was covered with hair when it was served. Her parents had called the facility as soon as they received the letter. I laughed out loud at hearing her story and promptly wrote to my parents about the hair on the food we were forced to eat. Not only that, but they didn't give us silverware and we had to eat with our fingers. Mom and Dad just wrote back and told me to make sure I washed my hands before I went to the cafeteria. Little did I know that this was typical of the first letters home from most of the kids entering the program. My parents had been given copies of similar letters from parents with kids in the program. With the parents talking it wasn't long before they figured out we were rotating the complaint that got the biggest response from parent to parent. It was scary to see how all the parents were committed to their kids graduating the program. I didn't believe I had much to be concerned with because my parents had said they were committed to things my entire life, but never followed through.

At the end of my second month I was told to go to the office to see Ms Freeman, our senior mental health counselor. She was the one I had imagined as this big black mama with a scowling face. In reality she was this little petite, gorgeous, perfectly composed, eloquent Jamaican. She seemed to possess the ability to look into your soul and mind and know what you were thinking or feeling. She asked me to sit down and handed me a handful of official-looking papers. I began reading rather haphazardly until the words jumped out, 'extended guardianship.' It had been signed by a judge in Montana and it gave my parents custody of me for six months beyond my 18th birthday.

Angrily, I challenged Ms Freeman. 'What does this mean?'

She smiled slightly and replied, 'It means if you don't start working your program, completing your schoolwork, and start dealing with issues affecting your life, you are going to be here a very long time.'

I replied, 'They can't do this, I am going to be an adult. Ms Freeman simply said, 'You are an adult when the court says you are. At this point you have not proven to the court, your parents, or to yourself that you are capable of making decisions like an adult.'

I started crying and I continued to cry off and on for the next three days. Once again I felt the anger and fear that had been the basis of my choices since my early days at Whitefish High. I didn't want to change. It was too hard and it would take too long. What about all of my friends and everything? Life at home was going to go on without me and people would forget who I was. Besides I had worked hard to make all the hurt go away, now people wanted me to look at it all over again, their way. I decided not to do anything and just cocoon myself. What could they do if I just chose to sit and do nothing?

Two days later I received a letter from my dad telling me how they were planning another trip to Hawaii and life was really great at home. He closed the letter with, 'I love you; p.s. How is your program going?' How's my program going, is he kidding? They are going to Hawaii and I am sitting at a program. It was as if a light went on or something. I was just sitting.

I finally woke up one morning and resigned myself to make an effort to complete the program. It took a couple of weeks but I finally agreed to the terms, I signed the forms and I knew that if I was ever going to do anything with my life, I needed to start doing it now. I knew that I wanted to live and I had dreams that I wanted to achieve; now I just needed to believe in myself as much as those around me did. It was without a doubt the hardest decision I have ever made. I had to make the choice to live or die and I chose to live. From that day on my life continually improved. After a month had passed I made the decision to graduate the program. I would show my mom and dad it didn't matter what they did: I was going to do this for me.

Life at TB wasn't all work and there was fun to be had. It was a hot day and all of us girls had been pestering our senior staff, Ms Smith, to let us go in the pool for our physical education portion of the day. She finally agreed. Using the pool was a privilege that we only got to enjoy every so often because the boys also used the pool as well. We weren't to look at boys or they at us or we would receive consequences; so obviously they weren't about to let us use it together. It was so funny to think, here we were in Jamaica, a Caribbean paradise, essentially party central and we were expected to behave like nuns in a monastery. The few times we were able to sneak a peek at our male counterparts, it was almost a joke. Their uniforms made them look like UPS (United Postal Service) drivers with shaved heads. You couldn't tell if they were cute or not, because they all looked alike.

It was so refreshing to get to swim. The pool was a good size and had several unique features. My favorite was the little blue crabs that wandered up from the shore for swim time. I was one of the first to enter the pool as usual when I noticed that one of the little crabs had fallen in the water. I figured that the poor little thing must have not been able to get out, resulting in his demise. I decided to have a little fun with the dead creature. One of the girls was from the East Coast and, to put it lightly, was somewhat sheltered from the nature experience. She wasn't particularly fond of any of the Jamaican wildlife, especially the crabs. Naturally she was a perfect target.

I called her over and, while discreetly hiding my little blue treasure behind my back, as soon as she was within reach I showed her what I had found. She screamed so loud that it revived the little crab and it started moving. I wasn't prepared for the crab's miraculous recovery and I started screaming as well. Mrs Smith wasn't impressed with my prank and she awarded both of us consequences. It was one of the few consequences I thoroughly enjoyed receiving; each of us having to write the details of the crab resurrection just made it more funny. The East Coast girl and I laughed about the event whenever we got together; we were lucky not to have received more consequences due to our continuous laughter about the incident.

In the months that followed there were many days when I just wanted to throw it all away. One day when I was level four (achievement level), several of us girls were sitting around talking about life back at home. The memories of just hanging out, the parties, and the drugs that we used to do. I realized my mouth was watering and one of the girls said I looked like a dog salivating over a bone. The feeling terrified me and for the first time I realized what I had done to my life. It had been ten months since my last use and I was still feeling the same urges and cravings. The thought of what I had become and all that I did just to get my drugs made me sick to my stomach and I knew that I couldn't go back to the same place. I hated who I was and I was so scared that I might not be strong enough to stay clean. For the rest of my program I fought my fear of relapse. When I brought it up to my family their response was simple:

'You have a choice, Carren, no one can do it for you, not your family, not your friends, not your church. You can be clean and sober, or not, it is your choice.'

This became the basis of my life and I committed every part of my being to be clean and sober. No matter what, I had to do this and for me: this was my last chance!

It was November; I had been in the program for approximately nine months and was making significant progress understanding my addiction. I had joined a rape support group and finally shared with all the other girls the details of my first rape. I got angry at Stephen for what he had done to me; I would have probably killed him if he had been in the room. Eventually, that passed and I resigned myself to helping keep other young girls from becoming victims by scumbags like him.

Life was really good at the program. Mom and Dad had just visited me in October and our reunion was the best. I voluntarily signed permanent extended guardianship over to my parents until I graduated the program. It was a no-brainer as far as I was concerned. I wanted to graduate and if they were willing to keep paying the expenses, I could at least agree to the court order.

Foundation Family had changed since I first joined the group. I was a senior member now. I was level four and had earned the opportunity to be a mentor to new girls joining the family. A new girl had just come to the facility two days before and had been assigned to our family. She had been in several programs already and let us know in no uncertain terms that she was not going to participate in any way with anything this program had to offer. I remember looking at her face and seeing this overwhelming sense of hurt and despair. She was extremely withdrawn and refused to acknowledge our efforts at friendship.

We were sitting in class one day and she stood up and asked permission to throw a piece of paper in the trash container. The teacher granted her permission. She stood and then bolted for the open door. She ran past the two staff sitting at the door and jumped over the rail, falling three stories. She died immediately. All of us girls ran outside and looked over the rail to the ground below where she lay twisted and lifeless. Girls started crying and hysteria began to overcome the group in general.

For some reason I had this sense of calm and I knew I needed to calm the other girls. I gathered all the girls in the family and had them go inside. I calmed the girls down and reassured them it was going to be OK. I kept thinking back to the several attempts I had made to take my own life and realized how selfish I had been. That girl's family would never have the chance to hold her in their arms and tell her how much she meant to them. She was gone and they would have to live with the grief and emptiness created by her choices. I made a commitment to myself that day to honor life, not to take for granted the gift God had given me. I was going to graduate the program. There was going to be life for me after meth.

I finally got to level five and was able to enjoy all the privileges and benefits of success. The greatest experience of upper levels was getting to work outside the facility helping in the local elementary schools. We would get up early and several of us girls would act as aids in the classroom. I worked in the third grade class and had a great time helping the students read, complete crafts, and chaperone the playfield. I developed a new sense of respect for the opportunities America had in comparison to what was available to the typical Jamaican family. I began planning for my own future, something that not long ago I never expected to have. Helping others gave me the realization that I had a responsibility to others, as well as to myself. I loved life for the first time I could remember. Life – what a blessing. I am not going to waste one minute of it in the future.

With making level five I knew at any time my family would be returning to Jamaica for a family reunion. Mom and Dad had promised on their last visit, regardless of what it took, our family would be together again. I was helping out staff with some minor chores when I received a request from Ms Freeman to stop by the office after dinner to get the mail for our family. She said that there were also several things that she wanted to speak to me about. It was part of the usual routine and so as soon as I finished eating every grain of rice and peas, my favorite traditional Jamaican meal, I headed towards the office.

When I opened the door I thought that my eyes where playing tricks on me. I couldn't believe my entire family was standing right in front of me. Tears began pouring down my face and the faces of Mom and Dad, Alicia and Scott. I jumped into Scott's arms and grabbed Alicia at the same time. This was a dream come true – we were going to be a family again. I don't know how many hugs or tears were shared during our first time together in over a year, but I know in my heart I will never give up on myself or my family again.

I was given an off grounds pass for five days and told to enjoy my family. I knew there were apologies to be given, but regardless of what happened over the next few days, I knew we would always be a family.

The next day we had made plans to go to the beach. I was so excited that we were all together and I could not wait to show them how beautiful Jamaica was. As we walked to the overlook over the beach you could see for miles. We would be the only family picnicking on Treasure Beach today. We picked a nice spot under an almond tree and then broke out the snorkeling gear.

Scott and I ran into the water and began chasing all the multi-colored fish. It was as if we were little kids again back home at the White House, chasing butterflies. The fish were amazing and appeared to enjoy the game as much as we did. Alicia wanted to take a turn which surprised me because for as long as I could remember she was afraid the fish would bite her toes. We stayed in the fairly shallow water and close to a beautiful, brightly colored reef. It was fascinating to me how randomly the ocean floor changed from being only several feet deep in some locations and then suddenly dropping to great depths at others.

It was in one of the deeper parts that all of a sudden I felt myself being pulled backwards and under. My first thought was: *If this is a shark attack I'm not hurting as bad as I thought.* Suddenly I realized Alicia was pushing me under the water. She had seen a large fish under the water and in her panic to get away she made the decision to sacrifice whoever was close at hand. That just happened to be me. She had crawled up on my back so that she was almost entirely out of the water. Alicia jumped toward shore, freeing me to do the same. My thoughts at the time were sharks had nothing over Alicia when it comes to scaring the daylights out of someone in the ocean. We laughed and laughed at both of our reactions. It was great to be sisters again.

We continued to swim, take naps, talk, and play, just enjoying being a family again and spending time with each other.

It was such a wonderful time and I took the opportunity to apologize to my brother Scott and my sister Alicia for the problems I had created for them due to my drug use. It gave me such a warm feeling to be a family again and for the first time I realized in a few short months I would be graduating and heading home.

20. FAMILY REUNION

You don't choose your family. They are God's gift to you, as you are to them.

Desmond Tutu

It was mid January, our tickets were purchased, accommodations confirmed; we were embarking on a journey of uncertainty, everything to gain, a family to heal.

As we walked down the jetway at Glacier Park International Airport thoughts, memories, and anxieties seemed to mesh all into one. Our entire family had been affected by our daughter's choices of using meth and her attempts at suicide. It had been a year since we were all together. We had escorted Carren to Tranquility Bay, Jamaica over nine months ago. The months before in which she had been living on the streets had created a life of hell for all of us. Alicia fled home for college at Bozeman. Scott was still at home, overwhelmed and struggling. Karyl and I were just wondering how it all came to pass.

Seven months ago Alicia, embarrassed by her younger sister's actions, frustrated over her own life events, and angry with us for our failure as parents, stood screaming and crying, 'I am going to college, trying to make something out of my life. All the money you are wasting on Carren should be for my college. She is just trash; it will all be for nothing.'

Scott, currently in his junior year of high school, scared stiff as a result of the consequences Carren was suffering, was still trying to make sense of it all. Carren his older sister, his long ago sandbox buddy, sledding partner and confidant, was now gone. Kids at school berated him with accounts of her actions, calling her druggie, slippy, slut and whore. He has been hurt so deeply, his life was in the shadow of our efforts to save his sister Carren.

Karyl is quiet, praying for a miracle, always the eternal mother, an only child herself, not understanding the constant bickering between siblings. She believes the only chance for reconciliation will only come from God's intervention.

For me the flight created conflicts and concerns. The majority of my family was close at hand: Carren, safe, a great distance away. I felt I needed to put all my business and personal effects in order. My business supported so many and I wanted to ensure it continued. Most importantly we needed the assurance of Carren's well-being and provisions for her to complete the program.

Upon arrival in Montego Bay, we were met by Bunny, a new friend from a previous parent weekend, and taxi operator extraordinaire from Treasure Beach. We piled our luggage into the rear compartment of his Toyota Station Wagon, Alicia took shotgun, and off we went on 'Mr Toad's Wild Ride.' Four hours of too many cars, too little room, and too many potholes. This being our third trip to Jamaica, Karyl and I were convinced that Jamaican vehicles were manufactured with overactive car horns, no brakes and an uncontrollable accelerator. Through the course of the trip Alicia's once proud fingernail collection had disappeared and Karyl had permanent fingerprints implanted into the back of Bunny's seat.

We arrived at Tranquility Bay, Caribbean Center for Change at 4:30 pm. Our family visit with Carren wasn't scheduled to begin until the next day, but Bunny informed us that our family rep wanted to meet us prior to our reunion with Carren. We assumed that it was to establish the protocol for our visit, to set the ground rules, so to speak. We entered the reception area and received wonderful hugs and greetings from many of the staff that we had met on our October Parent Weekend.

We were visiting, discussing the eventful ride from Montego Bay to Treasure Beach, when the door from the pool area opened.

Alicia, our oldest daughter and Scott, our seventeen-year-old son, had their backs to the door and didn't notice who had entered. Only two feet away from each of them was their sister they hadn't seen for over a year. The family disintegration that had occurred had not been pleasant. Karyl and I just stood and watched, holding each other, tears running down our faces. It seemed forever before Carren's eyes adjusted to the interior light; she started to cry softly. Alicia and Scott turned around, and our three children were together once again. They all reached for each other at the same time. There were tears, and I love you, and I miss you, all at one time. Karyl and I held each other. Once again our children were sandbox buddies, queen-bed acrobats, a trio of forest explorers with juice packs and chips. A miracle had happened; our family was beginning to heal.

We spent four magnificent days visiting with Carren. There were many tears, challenges, and great love shared. It was not always pleasant, but always respectful. We all shared our experiences and Carren apologized individually to each of us, and each of us to her. Each day we would walk to a private little beach, where the rising tide had erased our previous day's activities. The sand was smooth and unmarred, reminding us that each day was a new beginning. We each shared our fears, hurts and dreams. We were a family again.

It was not easy for us to send our daughter 3000 miles away from home: A foreign country, where we had no control and no personal experience. It was, however, the right choice for Carren and our family. She is proud of her accomplishments and we are proud of her. She admits it has been tough and early on she would have given up and walked away, if she could. Was it worth it? I think so. The morning we left, I was holding my baby girl in my arms once again, both of us in tears and she whispered, 'Daddy, thank you.'

21. IN WAITING

Victims of rape involving drugs or alcohol often experience even more psychological trauma than other rape survivors do. They are extremely likely to blame themselves. At least 45% of rapists are under the influence of alcohol or drugs.

Violence against Women, Bureau of Justice Statistics,
US Dept of Justice

Our reunion in Jamaica was an experience of a lifetime for our entire family. The trip home was filled with joy and excitement; for the first time in a long while we had dreams and were making plans for the future. Karyl and I felt our family was healing; Carren would soon be graduating from her program and coming home. We had all committed to putting the hurt and distrust behind us. Carren was making great strides in her battle with her meth addiction. Carren's comment about having days where she didn't have urges to use meth was a huge sign of progress. We had learned to appreciate the little achievements because there had been none for a long time. Carren was finally excited about life and we were excited for her. She wanted to go to college and we took time to review catalogues and consider college options. She was planning on playing her violin again and possibly joining an orchestra. Simply put we were getting our daughter back.

Carren had joined a rape support group at Tranquility Bay and expressed her anger for putting herself in positions resulting in her rapes. More importantly she was angry with the rapist. She now openly discussed her rape by Stephen in her early days at Whitefish High School. She also shared how a drug dealer named 'Skids,' who dealt drugs out of a bar called Kegler's Lounge, had savagely beaten and raped her. It seems Skids liked the added excitement of having sex while his victims were bleeding from facial injuries he inflicted during the assault. She expressed repeatedly how she wanted to share her experience with other young women, hoping to prevent similar tragedies. Teen rape was on the rise in our community and Carren knew she could at least give other teens the insight not to put themselves in harm's way.

After arriving home we quickly got back to our routines. Scott was in his junior year at school having a great time. Karyl and I got back to work and despite the costs of Carren's program we seemed to have enough money left over to start helping Alicia with her college expenses. Our next phase in Carren's program would be a home pass, where Carren would fly back to Montana and be in our home for seven days. We had been advised this could be a rough experience for Carren and could trigger a lot of emotion and desire for drugs. It was a test to see how far she had come. Regardless, for our family and friends, it was a time to celebrate. Not too different than the story of the prodigal son in the Bible. Our prodigal little girl was coming home and we planned on making it the best homecoming ever.

Karyl had some concerns about many of the drug dealers that had been looking for Carren when she first went away. Would she be safe? Would we be safe? Do you think they will come looking for her? I had very little concern. After Carren entered her program I worked with the local drug task force teams and most of her dealers were in jail. The others must have got wind of what was happening and disappeared from town. The drug task force called it the cockroach syndrome – running for cover! In any event, I believed Carren and our family would be safe at least for a short visit.

Her home pass was scheduled to take place in June or July, some of the best days in the 'Last Best Place.' We had purchased the plane tickets and all of us had this glow, just a great feeling that the tragedy was ending. I was at work when I received a call from the

Health Department. One of my friends worked in the sexually transmitted disease section and Carren's name had come up during an interview with a subject that had tested positive for HIV. He was providing names of people he had had sex with over the course of the last couple of years and Carren's name had come up. Evidently, he saw the story in the newspaper about Carren and our family and made the connection. Some great sense of remorse had come over 'Skids' now that he had a disease that could end his life. I guess he wanted to make amends for his transgressions.

I was in shock at hearing the words: 'Carren might be infected with HIV and we need to have her tested as soon as possible.' I informed the health officials that Carren had been tested prior to her entering her first program. Wasn't that good enough?

'No, many times the antibodies don't show up for up to three months,' the county health official replied, and she strongly advised Carren should be retested. I told her Carren was coming home for her first home visit and we scheduled an appointment the day her flight arrived in Kalispell. We called Jamaica and talked to her psychologist and advised him of the information we had received. He suggested that we wait until she was home and share the information with her as a family

He encouraged us that there was a good chance she was not infected. 'Keep your hopes up, you will all be OK.'

It was hard not to let the thought of Carren with HIV get us down; we thought we were over the fear and hurt from our family's journey with meth.

Carren's flight came in and our entire family, as well as many family friends, were there to greet her. The hugs and joy were the best a dad could ask for. After securing the luggage we left the airport and took the scenic route home through the grain fields and along the Whitefish river. It was great to have Carren home. Once home we shared with Carren the information we had received. We were in tears expecting the same from her. Instead she gave us a hug stating, 'Mom and Dad, I may or may not have HIV: let's go do the test and find out. It was my choices that put me in this position. I can live with the outcome. This is my first time home with you in over a year. Let's not let something that happened a long time ago affect our visit. It is OK. I love you.'

Karyl stayed home to make dinner, Carren and I made the trip to Flathead County Health. As I sat in the waiting room, I looked around at the many young women waiting for their appointments.

There was such a sense of loss and failure on their faces. Many only in their early teens were pregnant. Others were obviously there to have the test for sexually transmitted diseases as well. It was not a happy place. I took out a piece of paper and started writing my thoughts.

'Today I sit, a father-in-waiting. My beautiful daughter, just 18 years, has come so far. She has beautiful eyes, soft hair, and a warming smile. Not long ago she chose not to live; now she longs for life. She is once again experiencing success in her life and has pride in her achievements. We are a family in healing and have shared great love. Yet today I sit a father in waiting; not to hear her play her violin, experience the pleasure of her marriage as we walk down the aisle, or to be blessed as a grandfather for the first time from her family of choice. The drug dealer that so violently raped my little girl is reportedly HIV positive. So we wait together, again, with an uncertain future. I am proud of my little girl. She has beautiful eyes, soft hair, and a warming smile. I love her so much, and my heart is breaking.'

The tests were completed; we would have to wait a couple of weeks for the results. Carren would be back in Jamaica by that time, so all we could do was wait.

Our seven-day visit with Carren was the best. The topic of HIV never came up again after the first day, and was not on any of our minds. The joy of being a family again, the love shared, walks in the forest, breathtaking sunsets, and glorious sunrises made the week perfect. Carren and I walked down the driveway one morning to get the mail. We both remembered the day she first went to the 'Big Kids' School.' As we walked down the timbered drive, she wrapped her arm around mine.

'Dad, I wish that I would have made different choices back then. I am sorry for the hurt it has caused you, Mom, Scott, and Alicia. When Collette and I cut school that day and went over to Stephen's, it just seemed like a fun thing to do. I wonder how many other kids are making the mistake I made.'

I didn't have an answer; I did suggest that when she graduated her program and finally came home, maybe she could ask kids in school the same question.

22. TEENS IN CRISIS: FOR PARENTS ONLY

You see the child whom you love, the happy healthy young man with a great future ahead of him, a talented athlete, a good student, a budding computer whiz, a generous loving friend, a new father, and he's losing everything to a drug. Every dollar he gets goes to buy drugs and party. He loses his job, his car is repossessed, his house is foreclosed, and his wife leaves him. The grief is unremitting, It's worse than death. Your formerly happy and generous child is replaced by a selfish, lying, evasive and suspicious monster. He gets violent and abusive toward you, threatens you and steals from you.

Mary F. Holley, MD, Crystal Meth – They Call It Ice

I began forming the idea of Teens in Crisis on the drive home from Salt Lake City. Just prior to boarding the plane for Jamaica, Carren asked me to find some way to help the other kids she had been hanging with. I remembered how Karyl and I felt completely alone, partly because we were so ashamed of our failure as parents. It would have been a great help if we could have had someone to talk to who had been there, done that. The traditional services were not available for families with kids in crisis unless their children had the opportunity to be arrested. Even when kids were put in the system there were no guarantees they would receive the proper treatment, counseling, or medical care necessary for meth abusers.

After returning home I again met with the Gardner family. They were still attempting to understand and cope with the death of their eighteen-year-old daughter (having battled unsuccessfully with her addiction, she had finally shot herself in the head). Gerri Gardner was learning all she could about her daughter's addiction to meth. I told Gerri Gardner how Carren had requested I do something to help other kids and their families going through the same tragedy we had experienced. Gerri and I agreed to start a support group, calling it Teens in Crisis. We planned to meet once a week and decided Thursday evenings had the fewest conflicts for families. We contacted the local police, hospitals, schools, and counseling centers, advising them of our newly created group.

For about three weeks we were the only ones sitting in the room. It gave us time to reflect on our children, what we could have done differently, what were other options: We called it the 'Could Haves, Should Haves and Would Haves.' Within a month families started to attend and it was immediately apparent meth was a big problem in the Flathead Valley.

Shortly after officially forming Teens in Crisis as a non-profit corporation and holding our first meetings, meth took another victim. Gerri's husband, Troy, just couldn't understand how meth was able to take his little girl from him. He fell into deep depression and made the decision to take his own life. He committed suicide sixteen months to the day after the death of his daughter. Karyl and I believed Gerri's loss of her daughter and husband would destroy her. By no means did we expect her to participate in the work of forming Teens in Crisis or attend the weekly support group meetings. Amazingly, a week after her husband's funeral, Gerri showed up at our Thursday night meeting and announced, 'Meth has taken two members of my family. Enough is enough! It is my intention to do whatever it takes to stop any other families from losing their children or any family member to meth.' We became intensely committed to our goal of 'Making a Difference One Life at a Time.'

I often look back and long for those early days when we wondered if anyone would ever attend the support meetings. Currently, we have 30–40 families per week in attendance. Our phones ring constantly from parents experiencing horrible crisis behaviors from their children. Just when we think things can't get any worse as far as children's behaviors and choices are concerned, reality slaps us in the face with more tragedy.

One single mother with a fourteen-year-old girl involved in meth attended our meeting for support. She had attempted to get her daughter arrested due to her abuse of meth but to no avail. She wanted her little girl to go into treatment of some form or another but she didn't have the financial means to pay for treatment. As a group we had no funds and advised the mom to see if there were family members, out of the area, where her daughter could live.

Within a week her daughter had run away again and died of an overdose of meth and alcohol. It was apparent that teen suicide, rape, overdose, and an ever-increasing list of drugs of abuse – methamphetamines, heroin, prescription drugs, marijuana, alcohol, mushrooms, LSD, cocaine, huffing (breathing paint fumes) and dusting (inhaling contents from compressed air dusting containers i.e. computer air cleaners) – were taking a horrible toll on our children. As a group, Teens in Crisis committed their efforts to raise money to assist families who normally could not afford expensive drug and mental evaluations, intervention, or residential treatment. To sit by idly and give in to the fact that if you don't have enough money your children aren't worth saving was intolerable.

Months of support group meetings, with hundreds of families experiencing their children in crisis behaviors, brought a sense of clarity to all the regular participating members. It became obvious that the crisis facing America's teens was not solely a police problem. A tremendous breakdown was occurring in families and clearly parents from all walks of life were either in denial that problems existed or justified their children's behaviors based on their past life experiences. Many parents minimized their children's involvement with marijuana and alcohol as a rite of passage stating: 'That's what we did as kids and we turned out OK.' What they failed to realize was 'times are different.' Teen suicide rates are up, emergency room admissions are up due to drug and alcohol abuse, traffic fatalities where alcohol is involved are up, teen addiction to drugs and alcohol are up, admission of children to rehabilitation and behavioral modification programs are up, diagnoses for teen depression are up and teens actively participating in sexual activities are up.

All too often we characterize this breakdown of social values as a direct result of economic status; however, the reality of this new epidemic of crisis behaviors practiced by American youth transcends all social, economic, and ethnic boundaries. In the case of meth, for example, Wendy Ostrom Price, a popular newscaster for KOFI radio, Kalispell, Montana, boldly proclaims, 'Meth is an equal opportunity destroyer.' That same statement can be made about most of the at risk behaviors practiced by our children today. We are losing a valuable American resource: our children. Unfortunately, many parents, grandparents, brothers and sisters, aunts and uncles, and families in general have yet to come to this realization.

One year after we formed Teens in Crisis, Senator Max Baucus, Montana, visited the Flathead Valley to assist the community and focus their efforts on battling the meth epidemic. After conducting an extensive survey of students at local schools, Senator Baucus suggested using teens in recovery to share their experiences with their peers. Teens in Crisis started the Kids Talking to Kids program in light of Senator Baucus's efforts. Carren, just home from graduation, along with five other students from Spring Creek Academy in Thompson Falls participated in the first presentations in Great Falls, Wolf Point, Harlem, Butte, Miles City, Terry, and Colstrip, Montana. Since that first series of talks, student graduates from Teen Challenge, Spring Creek Lodge, Big Sky Youth Home, Hope Ranch, Tranquility Bay, SUWS, Connection Corrections, and Cross Creek Academy have shared their life's stories with thousands of Montana students and parents.

This new epidemic called meth is real and is taking our children's lives at an unprecedented rate. Most in the narcotics enforcement business expect the meth epidemic to last at least another 12–15 years unless something drastic happens to alter the current course of events. Watching the course of other drugs of abuse and the impacts on user communities, there are two paths this current epidemic can take. The first is the law of attrition and is the current policy in practice throughout the nation. This policy is simply that, given time, the overwhelming death and decimation created by meth will naturally instill hesitancy by users to participate in the use of the drug, meth. This is a risky course to embark on, due to the sustained nature of abuse by users.

In Hawaii, where meth use is approaching its twentieth year since widespread introduction, usage is continuing to increase. Families are passing on the tradition of meth abuse to their children and extended families. There does not appear to be any significant reduction in first time users. The second alternative is that – as parents, families, communities, and as a nation – we take a stand not to allow the insanity of methamphetamine use to continue. We implement policies, behavioral limits, and expectations for our children that will alter their pursuit of dangerous behaviors.

Teens in Crisis in support of parents, has adopted a series of standards that must be provided for children to create an opportunity for success. We call this a Life Contract and it should encompass the following:

1. Love your children unconditionally
2. Provide adequate food and shelter for your children to allow full growth and development.
3. Set clear and understandable limits, based on your family values. Remember family values are followed at home and away by all members of the family.
4. Establish pre-agreed consequences for children's behaviors that do not conform to your family values. Consequences do not encompass abuse.
5. Allow your children to experience natural consequences for their choices and behaviors. As long as the experience is not life threatening, it provides them with the opportunity to learn from their mistakes.
6. You are responsible for who your children are, not what they do!
7. Provide the opportunity for your children to attend school that will support your values and facilitate their success in an adult world.
8. Don't lie to your children. For example if you make plans to participate with your children in an event (dinner, sports, working in the yard, reading activity), don't break your agreement for more important pressing issues. You minimize your children's value and have broken your agreement.
9. Respect adult relationships, commitments and agreements. When you have children they expect you to be there for them as a family. Each parent should respect each other and honor that commitment. If the grass seems greener on the other side of the fence, it is because someone is committing more effort and care for their yard than you are yours.
10. Be involved in your children's lives by knowing their friends, their friends' parents, where your children are, and what they are doing.
11. Reduce children's involvement with television and video games. TV should be limited to a maximum of one hour per day and should be utilized as a family activity and programs should support your family values.

12. Commit your family to regular religious activities. If faith-based options are not part of your values, then commit to outdoor activities, exercise or other committed activities that can be done as a family.
13. Eat dinner at home as a family at least three nights per week. During dinner do not allow outside interruptions during this family event. Disconnect the phone, no TV, no guests – this is time for your family to share your lives, experiences, and at times frustrations.
14. Minimize the amount of cash accessible to your children. Provide only the amount necessary for daily food or transportation requirements. Let them earn the rest.

Each of these items has been proved effective in reducing teens' participation in at risk behaviors. Your children are worth your effort and commitment. It is your responsibility to set your children up for success. Our children's lives are too important to waste.

Throughout America we are at a defining moment. As responsible citizens, communities, and a nation we need to take steps to prevent the loss and degradation of our children. The following practices should be implemented immediately to build healthy and safe communities for our children:

1. Join together to assist families experiencing crisis.
2. Assist single-family households with emotional and financial support as needed.
3. Provide support for agencies that are primary responders and support agencies for our kids in crisis.
4. Challenge our judicial agencies to take decisive steps to eliminate dangerous offenders from our communities.
5. Implement comprehensive education concerning the dangers of alcohol, drugs, and at risk behaviors that will give our children and grandchildren the information allowing them to make choices today that they can live with tomorrow.
6. Commit to volunteer community service. Each of us has a responsibility to help each other. All too often we make excuses or wait for the other person to take the initiative.
7. Implement random drug testing in schools.

We have lost too many children to suicide, drug abuse, murder, violent behavior, and alcohol-related deaths. The statistics make shocking reading:

1. TEEN SUICIDE

Suicide is now the second leading cause of death for teens throughout the United States – *it is an epidemic.* If depressive illnesses are left untreated, they can be fatal. Approximately 30,000 people kill themselves in the United States each year. Because of inaccurate reporting (such as recording a suicide as an accident), researchers suggest that the actual figure may be three times higher than this.

National Suicide Hot Line

- Each year 5000 teenagers and young adults kill themselves.
- Teen suicides have increased since the 1950s.
- The suicide rate for 15–19 year olds was higher than it had ever been approaching the 1990s.
- Frequently, case workers find that suicidal youths did not intend to die from their attempted suicide.
- For every two victims of homicide in the US there are three deaths from suicide.
- There are now twice as many deaths due to suicide than due to HIV/AIDS.
- More teenagers and young adults die from suicide than from cancer, heart disease, AIDS, birth defects, stroke, pneumonia and influenza, and chronic lung disease, combined.

2. DRUG ABUSE

Among the substances abused are: alcohol, tobacco, marijuana, cocaine, opiates, 'club drugs' (ecstasy, etc.), stimulants (methamphetamines, etc.), hallucinogens, inhalants, prescription drugs, and steroids.

Drug and substance abuse among teenagers is substantial. Among youths aged 12–17, about 1.1 million meet the diagnostic criteria for dependence on drugs, and about 1 million are treated for alcohol dependency.

Almost two-thirds of all American young people try illicit drugs before they finish high school. One out of 16 seniors smokes marijuana daily and 20 percent have done so for at least a month sometime in their lives. A recent poll found that adolescents listed drugs as the most important problem facing people their age, followed by crime and violence in school and social pressures.

Drugs have changed the social landscape of America. Street gangs spring up nearly overnight looking for the enormous profits drugs can bring. Organized crime is also involved in setting up franchises that would make McDonald's envious. But these are not hamburgers. In the world of drugs, homicidally vicious gangs compete for market share with murderous results. Many gang members outgun the police with their weapons of choice: semi-automatic pistols, AK-47s, and Uzis. Drug dealers have also gone high tech using cellular phones and computers to keep track of deals, while their teenage runners wear phone beepers in school.

National Youth Network (http://www.nationalyouth.com/substanceabuse.html)

The Parents' Resource Institute for Drug Education (PRIDE) reports that children who abuse illicit drugs are significantly more likely to carry a gun to school, take part in gang activities, think of suicide, threaten harm to others, and get in trouble with the police than children who abstain.

3. MURDER AND VIOLENT BEHAVIOR

Teens that commit acts of serious violence are often involved in other types of criminal behavior and live a lifestyle that involves a number of risky behaviors, including using drugs, carrying weapons, driving recklessly, and having unsafe sex (www.safeyouth.org).

While some violent teens begin to get in trouble as children, most don't become involved in a violent lifestyle until their teenage years (www.safeyouth.org).

Researchers have identified some factors that increase children and teens' risk for becoming involved in serious violence during the teenage years. For children under 13, the most important factors include: early involvement in serious criminal behavior, early substance use, being male, a history of physical aggression toward others, low parent education levels or poverty, and parent involvement in illegal activities (www.safeyouth.org).

One national survey found that for every teen arrested, at least 10 were engaged in violence that could have seriously injured or killed another person.

A review of surveys found that between 30–40% of male teens and 16–32% of female teens say they have committed a serious violent offense by the age of 17.

Older teens and young adults (18–24 years old) experienced the highest homicide victimization rates, a change from the late 1970s when 25–34-year-olds had the highest rates (Bureau of National Statistics).

4. TEEN ALCOHOL ABUSE

Teen alcohol problems create many negative consequences including car accidents (drinking and driving), physical fights, homicides, suicides, falls and toxic poisoning to name a few. One of the deadliest outcomes of teenage alcohol abuse is drinking and driving. Car accidents are the leading killer of the 15–20-year-old age group.

Alcohol abuse increases the rate of teen dating violence. According to the National Institute on Alcohol Abuse and Alcoholism (NIAAA), 'Among college students under age 21 alone, 50,000 experience alcohol-related date rape, and 430,000 are assaulted by another student who has been drinking.'

The definition of insanity is doing the same thing over and over, expecting different results: We can make the choice to stop the insanity. Let's leave a legacy to our children and grandchildren that we can be proud of. Let's not leave our children with a lifetime of regret brought on by the horrific forces of addiction, sexual abuse, rape, and sexually transmitted diseases.

23. FOR KIDS ONLY

You are worried about seeing him spend his early years in doing nothing. What! Is it nothing to be happy? Nothing to skip, play, and run around all day Long? Never in his life will he be so busy again.

Jean-Jacques Rousseau, Emile, 1762

There are some things I want you to know. First, I promise I will not lie to you, nor will I make any attempt to scare you for the purpose of altering your behavior. This chapter will provide you with information based on education, observations, and experience from a wide range of youth and adults. It will at times be harsh and graphic, but it is an honest effort to provide you with information you deserve to know.

Over the past five years I have had the opportunity to work with thousands of students of all ages. In the fall of 2001, Senator Max Baucus came to the Flathead Valley to talk to students at our schools. He came primarily because he was concerned about Montana's students and wanted to know what he could do to assist in providing information that would help students make better, informed, decisions. During the course of his visit he conducted a student survey with one of the questions focusing on how best to provide information to students.

Students responded unanimously; they are tired of being lectured to! They want to hear real life experiences from kids that have 'been there, done that.' With that request and the assistance of Senator Baucus's office, Gerri Gardner (whose daughter committed suicide battling her meth addiction) and I started the Kids Talking to Kids program. I met with several directors of Therapeutic Boarding Schools and asked if they would make students available that were attending their schools, to speak with students throughout Montana. Spring Creek Lodge Academy, Thompson Falls, Mt. Big Sky Youth Home, Columbia Falls, Mt., and Hope Ranch, Whitefish, Mt. agreed to provide students preparing to graduate the opportunity to share their experiences.

Since that time I have made hundreds of appearances and spoken to thousands of parents and students around Montana and South Dakota. Throughout the course of this chapter I want to share with you some of the life choices of some of the students that participated and the efforts to regain their lives.

The first thing I learned from listening to these students share their lives is that none of them ever expected to become alcoholics, drug addicts, rapists, prostitutes, thieves, or be arrested for felonies that would affect their lives forever. Not one ever planned on participating in behaviors that would result in the loss of the life of their very best friends. None ever expected to have sexually transmitted diseases, or to never be able to have children. But in fact that was the result of their choices.

Matt was sixteen years old when I first met him. He had been attending a residential boarding school for about thirteen months. Matt was a recovering meth addict and an alcoholic. This was the first time he had ever publicly spoken about his involvement in drugs, alcohol, and crime. As I introduced Matt to the high school assembly he boldly stepped forward and made a simple statement before sharing the story encompassing the last three years of his life.

'I had a lot of opportunities to do things different. It was my choice to use alcohol and drugs and I have no one to blame for those choices but me.' Matt started using alcohol when he was twelve years of age. By age thirteen he was using marijuana at least three times a day. By his sophomore year he had been arrested for assault, theft, and possession of dangerous drugs. His parents continually found ways to get Matt out of trouble, but never once confronted him about his choices. Matt began selling drugs to support his drug habit and within a year had supplied drugs to his

FOR KIDS ONLY

best friend which resulted in his death. Matt was sixteen when he was finally escorted to a Behavioral Modification School. He fought and screamed the entire way there. Matt concluded his life story by simply stating the words: 'choices, my choices.'

In fact, life is a series of choices. Every day you make choices concerning your future. Neither your teacher, your parents, nor any authority figures have the ability to stop you from making these decisions. If you want independence, you can have it. On a daily basis you have the ability to make choices affecting the rest of your life. You can choose whether to eat or not to eat; the latter resulting in anorexia or bulimia. You can decide whether to do school work or not – 'not' resulting in the ultimate removal from school either by dropping out or expulsion. You can use alcohol or not; it is most often readily available within the home or from friends. You can choose to use a myriad of drugs whether prescription or illicit, or participate in a world of at risk behaviors. There is nothing anyone can do to make you choose one way or the other. However, before you make the choices to use alcohol or drugs, have sex, or participate in other life altering behaviors, you should have all the information available to assist you in your decision process.

My experience with adults is that they are all too willing to allow TV or movies the opportunity to provide information about sex, alcohol, or drug use. However, they are either unwilling, do not have time, or are fearful of presenting this information to you themselves. When the decision is finally made to enlighten you, they spend time telling you what they think you should hear rather than sharing honestly their personal experiences and life consequences. We often justify not telling you the truth, thinking that the truth is too harsh or not age appropriate. I hear parents constantly making the excuse that telling kids about drugs, alcohol, and sex will only expand their curiosity and accelerate their interest. Often we do not have adequate information, are unwilling, or emotionally un-prepared to relate information about subjects related to sexual behavior, alcohol or drug use.

Michelle was thirteen when she met a friend on the Internet. She immediately found someone that was willing to listen to her and take an interest in her daily life. His name was Chad and although he was two years older than she was, she was convinced no harm would come from expanding the friendship. Anyway her mom and dad both worked and never seemed to be at home. Even though she had an older brother and a younger sister, she felt she was alone.

169

Over the course of the next three months Michelle spent every day talking with Chad on the computer. She wanted desperately to meet with him, have dinner and get to know him better. She finally agreed to meet with him in the city near where they lived. The location was a hotel with a restaurant on the main floor. She was to go to the room number he had given her and knock and they would get dressed and go to dinner. She knocked on the door and was never given the opportunity to have dinner that evening.

Michelle was repeatedly raped by a man in his mid forties. His name wasn't Chad and everything he had said about himself was a lie. She felt so ashamed and stupid for making the choice to meet with him. She had lied to her parents about where she was going that evening and now she had to live with the choice she had made. Within two months Michelle was using meth on a daily basis. She started prostituting to pay for her drug habit and attempted suicide twice. She was constantly running away and had contracted sexual transmitted diseases (STDs). As far as she was concerned her life wasn't worth living.

When Michelle related her story to students in Hamilton, Montana she had been in a program for over thirteen months. I will never forget her closing comments to the students: 'I have learned to forgive myself for my choices, I only hope that someday I will be able to find someone who will love me regardless of what I have done.'

As a father, I will always hold myself responsible for not being able to protect Carren from the rape inflicted on her by Stephen. It is a father's duty to protect their children; isn't it? Actually, what I realize now is that as a father, I am responsible for who my children are, but not for what they choose to do. That is important for you to realize as well. Your choices are your own. With that said it is also important for you to realize that your youth and innocence have made you a commodity to many of the human predators lurking in our communities, towns, and cities. A predator by definition is a creature that lives on the flesh of another. There are a significant number of these types of predators that are seeking both young boys and girls. Most often they do not appear dangerous, and most commonly use your classmates to lure you into their world.

Jennifer was twelve when she started playing with the neighbor boy that lived cross corner to the rear of their home. They had just moved into the neighborhood two months before and hoped she would be able to make friends before school started in the fall. Richie had lived with his dad since his parents divorced last year. They had a nice home and soon her parents and Richie's dad became friends. It wasn't long before Jennifer was spending a lot of time at Richie's house. Richie's dad always had treats in the fridge and occasionally would allow them to have a drink of his beer. Jennifer remembered Richie's dad telling them not to tell her parents or it would make them mad. It was only a little beer after all.

After six months had passed, along with Jennifer's thirteenth birthday, Richie offered Jennifer some marijuana.

'Oh, I don't do drugs,' was Jennifer's first reply.

'This isn't drugs, it's only marijuana,' Richie responded. 'My dad and I use it all the time. Here, I will light it up and show you how to smoke it; you just kind of suck in air along with putting it to your lips.'

'I don't know,' Jennifer replied. 'I promised not to use drugs when I was in DARE.'*

'Yeah and you also promised not to drink,' Richie responded quickly, 'but you drink beer, wine and other stuff my dad gives you. Come on it will be fun!'

Jennifer relented and tried her first hit on marijuana three weeks after turning thirteen. Before long, additional drugs were being offered and used. One evening while Richie's dad was watching Jennifer while her parents were out for the evening, Richie's dad provided a lot of alcohol, marijuana and cocaine for their use. It was a fun party until Richie's dad undressed Jennifer and had sex with her. She didn't know what to do to stop him and even if she had tried she was so high she knew she could not have. He warned her not to tell her parents about what had happened because they would blame her for using drugs and alcohol. Anyway, who would they believe – him or her.

Over the next few months Richie's dad used her on a weekly basis. He would even get her high and let his friends use her at will. He started telling her he loved her and wanted to marry her. What amazed Jennifer was she actually started to believe what he was telling her. Regardless, as long as he gave her all the drugs and alcohol she wanted, what did it matter anyway? She was used goods and no one would ever want her now anyway.

---

* Drug Abuse Resistance Education – Government education program provided in schools beginning in fifth grade; originally created by Glen Levant, LAPD, as a continuous program beginning in the first grade through twelfth grade. Due to budget considerations this is only offered in fifth grade.

Jennifer was fourteen and a half when she attempted suicide the first time. She hated her life, hated her parents, and hated school. The only way she knew how to get out was to take her own life. After telling her story to students at Columbus High School, Jennifer was asked to meet with some of the other girls from the school who had been raped by family members and friends. It was the same story but a different book.

The drug business is just that – business. Although it is your friends and acquaintances that most often introduce you to your first walk on the edge, somewhere there is someone making money on your decision to use. They have no conscience about whether you live or die as a result of your choice. To them it is strictly about money!

Alise planned on attending college, possibly becoming a doctor some day. She was bright and dedicated toward her school efforts. Her family took pride in her achievements at school and had been saving money since Alise's entrance into this world for her college. Alise was now seventeen years old and had already undergone an abortion. Meth had become the most important thing in her life and she was willing to do anything to get the drug that controlled her life.

She lived with three older men not far from the high school and it was her job to get high schoolers to come by and purchase drugs from her suppliers. She was called a recruiter by the drug task force and her job was to maintain a steady supply of new users from the local high school. She had been bringing kids from school for almost the entire year. It was impossible to count how many kids now used her suppliers to support their own drug habits. They didn't use her for sex any longer. She was used up as far as they were concerned plus they now had an endless supply of younger girls to use in exchange for drugs, alcohol, and money. If some of the younger boys wanted sex she was often directed to put out or she wouldn't be privy to any more freebies to support her habit. She was a long way from attending college or ever becoming a doctor.

It was a year ago she tried meth for the first time. The school year ended and she had been at the mall, shoplifting a new outfit. Plus she could often find new recruits to bring by to try some of her suppliers' goods. As she walked up to the door, the house seemed strange. The door was partially open and when she entered, the house was completely empty. There was some trash on the floor, but the sparse amount of furniture and the three men she had lived with and worked for over the last twelve months were gone. She never saw the men again. She stayed at the empty house for a couple of days and then her need for drugs prompted her to find a new dealer. Her work relationship ended up being the same.

'You put out, shut up and do what you're told and I will keep you in supply of what you can no longer live without.'

All too often first time use happens when you make the choice to first try alcohol. Keggers are big in rural areas as well as in cities. I know most kids don't go to these impromptu gatherings searching for meth. My recent opportunity to talk to kids involved in programs was at Big Sky Youth Home in Columbia Falls, Montana. One sixteen-year-old recovering meth user was attending a kegger with a group of her girlfriends. She was offered a little pot; her friends said it was OK, it would just get you a little high. Unfortunately her joint was laced with meth (they dip the joint in liquid meth and then let it dry out before smoking).

Her high was so intense that she began searching out more of the supercharged pot. Within a month she had progressed to smoking meth from a pipe several times a day. She was getting her meth from one of her new friends that had also attended the kegger where she was first introduced to meth. She didn't have enough money to support her drug habit so she began stealing, dealing or screwing to get what she desperately needed. Fortunately, her parents finally caught on to her drug abuse. She had lost a tremendous amount of weight and upon admission to her first treatment program was diagnosed with two different STDs. She had been clean and sober for over eight months and is glad to have her life back; however, there is a strong possibility that she will never be able to have children: tough consequences for poor choices.

The saying goes like this. 'Kids don't go to keggers looking for meth, but meth definitely goes to keggers looking for kids.' If you didn't open it yourself, make it yourself, or if your drink or cigarette has left your sight for the slightest instant, don't use it again.

You are the brightest and best generation to enter this democratic experience called the United States of America, yet the baby boomer generation is not leaving you with the best opportunity for success. We are either unwilling or unable to provide you with a safe environment for transitioning into adulthood. Because drugs were used when we were young, too many of us feel it is your right of passage to use as well. We all too often justify our lack of involvement in your lives as being due to our efforts to provide you with a 'better life than we had.'

The reality is: our time is the best gift we can give our children. As for adult lifestyle examples, consider this: I asked one of my class of students to watch television during prime time hours between 5:00 pm and 9:00 pm and record the advertisements presented during these hours. You can tell a lot about society by what merchandisers offer. The students split up and assigned different groups varying channels to watch. Here are the results based on their survey of advertisements:

1. The majority of adults must have degrading muscles and joints requiring medication.
2. Most men over 40 have erectile dysfunction (ED).
3. We cannot sleep without drug assistance.
4. We cannot eat without drug assistance due to intestinal problems.
5. If you can't afford it, use your credit card or borrow the money: you deserve to have whatever it is you want!
6. If you have bad credit, hire someone to help you get out of it.

As adults we are leaving you with a significant national debt, low cash reserves in savings, and a burgeoning population of seniors requiring nursing care. As youth inheriting our choices, you can and should be demanding more from us; us being the adults currently running this world. Tell your parents you want more of their time and less things. You don't want to inherit their debt or world conflicts. You want them to set an example of active involvement in the democratic process. And you want them to take time out of the day to participate in your learning activities. Education begins at home and every parent has the responsibility to participate in the activity that encompasses the majority of your children's waking hours – school.

It is your life. Make choices that give you the best opportunity to live life to the fullest. Choose friends that will support you in being the best you can be. And whether or not you like Mr Bill O'Reilly, take the advice provided in his book *Who's Looking Out for You*:

Self awareness is a must for those of us who want to fulfill our potential. Honest self examination should be a part of our daily routine. We all make mistakes, but as we've discussed, the folks who make the fewest errors usually wind up the happiest.

24. METH BACK IN OUR HOME: THE DOWER FACTOR

Good people do not need laws to tell them to act responsibly, while bad people will find a way around the laws.

Plato (427–347 BC)

It never entered my mind that starting Teens in Crisis would result in the ultimate break-up of our family. Teens in Crisis was my way of honoring the commitment I had made to Carren the day she boarded the plane to Jamaica en route to the Caribbean Center for Change at Tranquility Bay. I can remember her plea as if it were yesterday: 'Dad, can you do something to help my friends back home? There are so many of them that are using meth just like me.'

Teens in Crisis was supposed to be a support group for parents, to assist families get help for their kids in crisis, raise funds to help pay for counseling, intervention, and rehabilitation. Granted, we accomplished the task in great strides, but I never realized by helping parents we would become a major resource of information about the types of narcotics being circulated, drug dealers, pimps, prostitution rings, child molestation and sexual abuse.

Every Thursday, parents would attend the group, different faces but similar stories: thirteen-year-old girls running off with 35-year-old men; being used for prostitution in exchange for drugs. Sons being raped by predators using date rape drugs; fearing making reports due to the trauma inflicted on victims during court trials; young daughters being molested and eventually turning to drugs, alcohol, or suicide. Parents would come bearing a wealth of names, phone numbers, and places in which their children were participating in horribly dangerous behaviors. Information on thefts, burglaries, and even murders was shared and we passed that information on to the appropriate police agencies. Our contact with the Kalispell Police Department, Flathead County Sheriffs Office, Northwest Drug Task Force, State Drug Enforcement Bureau and FBI became regular events.

There were dangers associated with our efforts. Druggies (parents typically refer to these children as someone else's kids), their dealers, and other criminal types, figured out that if parents came to our group it wouldn't be long before their kids would get some kind of treatment, counseling, or enrollment in a residential treatment; and the information on their activities would be made readily available to various police agencies. Many of the core members of the Teens in Crisis group started receiving threatening or bizarre phone calls which most often were shrugged off as nothing more than idle threats.

There was some humor that came about due to our tenacious activities. One couple told their daughter they were attending Teens in Crisis Support Group and asked her if she had heard of the group. She replied, 'Oh yeah, that is where parents go when their kids are acting up. Then the kids just disappear.' She followed up her reply: 'Am I going somewhere too?' They were honest and said if she didn't change her behaviors, they were considering that as an option. Over the course of the next several weeks the parents implemented a life contract and their daughter made the decision to get her life back on track. Our response: do whatever works to save your kids!

In early March 2003, parents started sharing information about a prominent Montana business man named Dale Dower. This immediately became personal because Dale was a friend of mine from my church. One of the parents attending the group for the first time asked to speak with me in private after the meeting. She asked if we had heard of Dale Dower. I said, sure I go to church with him right here at Trinity. He is a multi-millionaire and one of the most prominent community leaders in the State of Montana. She said no, not in the context of church or community activities. 'Is he involved in drugs?'

This mom had been attending the group to find out ways to get her daughter off meth. Her daughter had been a straight 'A' student and had a full ride academic scholarship to a prominent western university. Her daughter was introduced to meth over the summer at a party with friends and was now on the run, living on the streets, dealing, stealing and screwing for her next hit of white death – methamphetamines.

I related to her that I knew Dale Dower and that I doubted he had any affiliation with drugs, especially methamphetamines. I asked what made her think Mr Dower was involved in drugs and she became defensive and stated she had heard her daughter mention his name during a conversation with one of her drug buddy friends just before leaving home.

I told her I hadn't heard his name come up in those types of circles and told her maybe it was due to his connection with Christian Financial Concepts; a counseling and philanthropic organization started by Mr Dower to assist needy families. The mom replied that all she knew was that it sounded to her like Mr Dower was a source for drugs, regardless of his prominent standing in the community. I promised the mom that I would ask around quietly to parents and police agencies and see if they had heard anything about Mr Dower.

The next day I called one of my contacts on the Northwest Drug Task Force and asked if he had heard the name Dale Dower and if his name had come up in any investigations involving methamphetamines or other drug activity. He stated he hadn't heard anything personally, but he would check with the other investigators and agencies and see what he could come up with. He promised to get back to me by the end of the week with any information.

True to form, his response came a few days later. 'No, as far as anyone knows, he is just some rich guy that likes to help people out.' I thanked him for his efforts and decided to put the notion to rest. There is no way Dale Dower, an elder of my church, prominent civic leader, respected business man, dedicated family man and grandfather, could ever be involved in the horrors created by drug abuse or by meth.

The interesting aspect of Teens in Crisis was the change over of families. Although we met every Thursday night, the group continued to grow. Every week there were different families, different problems; kids running away, rapes, suicide attempts and successes, drug abuse – mostly meth – and alcohol abuse. Kids were overdosing, dying, and running away on a regular basis and yet life away from the group appeared to be normal. I would walk away after group and wonder how the community could tolerate such devastation to our youth, yet life went on like nothing was wrong.

It was one of those nights after group and I was trying to understand exactly what had taken place. One family's daughter had just run away; she was fifteen and had run away with a girlfriend. They were headed for Las Vegas to be with her 38-year-old boyfriend she had met on the Internet. We had over 30 parents that evening and each story was just as troubling. One new mom attending the group shared that her meth abusing daughter was getting her drugs from a business man here in the community named Dale Dower.

I sat up straight in my chair, looked at the mom and asked her to repeat what she had just said.

'My daughter is getting her drugs from Dale Dower and she is also getting money from him.'

I asked if she was sure and she replied, 'I found checks with his name on them in my daughter's room.'

'Maybe her daughter was getting help from his Christian Counseling Foundation,' I replied.

'The only help she is getting from him is money,' she said, ' in return for providing sex to him and his friends.'

Other members in the group asked how she knew this and she quickly responded, 'Because my daughter's friend is doing the same thing. She is also using meth and she told her mom she gets drugs from Mr Dower as long as she gives sex to him and his friends.'

I asked if she had any proof to back up her information and she told us that the other mom had checks and letters she found in her daughter's room that supported her information. I looked at all the other parents; they were staring incredulously at this mom and again repeated the importance of confidentiality. The mom that was relaying all the information asked if I would go to the police and see what I could do to start an investigation and I agreed. I also told her to get all the evidence together so the police could take a look at it. She said her only concern was getting her daughter off meth. If it took throwing a prominent churchgoing civic leader in jail then so be it. She wanted her daughter back.

The following day I contacted a member in our church for advice. We had known each other for many years and were long-time friends. Admittedly this was presenting a considerable problem for me personally. My family had gone to Trinity Church with the Dower family for years; we knew their children and considered ourselves family friends. He was in fact a prominent leader within our congregation and had provided counseling and mentor support to several families that attended the Teens in Crisis Support Group. The friend I was meeting with was also an elder of our church and a long-standing friend of Dale Dower. I began relating the information I had received over the past few months and he just sat and stared at me with a look of disbelief.

'Ron, do you think this is for real? I mean Dale is a leader in the community, our church, a powerful businessman; maybe these are people that just have a grudge against him.'

I replied I didn't know for sure, but these mothers say they have proof and have indicated that there are many, many more girls, all meth addicts, involved with Dale. We agreed to keep our meeting confidential and that I should take the information to the police. We were having support group the following day and I decided to see if any other information developed concerning Dale Dower's activities before going to the police. I also felt I should check with the other core members of the group and see what they felt should be done.

The Teens in Crisis group meeting the following night was packed with families in crisis, again with repeated stories of unbelievable life-threatening behaviors involving their children: Twelve year olds addicted to meth, running away leaving their parents in panic, grandparents taking custody of their grandchildren due to the parents' involvement in meth, overdoses and suicide attempts. One set of grandparents had just learned their grandchildren were being traded out for sex to drug dealers in exchange for meth. Their world had been shattered. They were now raising the grandchildren and they wanted help saving their son and daughter-in-law. It was a crisis evening all around, yet typical of Thursday night support group meetings these days.

There were two new families attending the meeting that evening that related their daughters were involved with Dale Dower and wanted to know what they could do to get their children off meth. By this time I had met with over five families that had related essentially the same story; daughters were meth addicts, were providing sex to Dale Dower for meth and money. After the meeting one mother came up to me and gave me an envelope and whispered that these were the names her daughter had given her. She said these people were all in attendance at a party in West Valley hosted by Dale Dower. She added that her daughter said there were many of Dower's friends there as well and that her daughter admitted they provided sexual services for drugs and money. All the girls had been paid by Dale Dower.

I met with core members of the group later that evening and advised them of the current information and that I was planning on going to the police. I hadn't opened the envelope as of yet and decided I should do it with witnesses present from the group. Written on the enclosed paper were names of prominent members of the community. When the mom had given me the note, she advised me there were more names if we wanted them. I thought, 'Crap, this is enough.'

The members of the group were stunned and we all wondered what to do. I finally suggested that I had worked with FBI agents on other matters and due to the sensitive nature of the information I thought I should bring them into this. Although in disbelief and stunned by the information, we all agreed that would be the best plan. I explained it was all secondhand information and as of yet we had no way of knowing whether this was true or not. I asked the group not to reveal any information until I had a chance to talk to the FBI.

The next day a corps group member (Alice) and I were scheduled to meet with two recovering meth addicts, Randall and Stephanie (not their real names). They had participated in the Kids Talking to Kids Program several months past and had asked if they could do so again. I decided to share the paper I had received from the mom at group the previous night without revealing the nature or origin of the names. I wanted to know, based on their extensive knowledge of the drug world in Kalispell, if there was a chance that this was true.

We were meeting at a local restaurant in Kalispell and as they sat down I handed them the paper and asked what they knew about the names on the paper. Their faces washed of all color and I thought Steph was going to faint. They immediately stood up and walked from the restaurant. Alice looked puzzled and asked what was going on. After a few minutes, Randall and Steph returned to the table and started sharing their story.

They admitted they were personally involved with Mr Dower. Steph was sexually involved with Mr Dower and Randall was providing drugs to other girls who were sexually involved with Mr Dower. They admitted they had needed money desperately and Dale Dower seemed an easy way to get it. They wanted to share all this information with the police but stated law enforcement officials were involved and with the recent unsolved murder of one of the Dower girls, they were afraid for their lives. Throughout the rest of the lunch they shared more of their involvement with Dale Dower which confirmed prior information received from other families that had attended the Support Group over the last few months.

Alice sat quietly listening to the story unfold, occasionally looking over at me in disbelief at what she was hearing. I advised Randall and Steph that I could put them into a safe house until we could get FBI investigators to come in from out of town to conduct interviews. They agreed and we put in motion our standard safe house placement. I advised them they would be kept in a safe place, out of town, for a few days until the FBI were available.

'What have you gotten us involved in?' Alice said after the meeting.

'A real mess,' I replied, 'and I am sorry.'

Two days later FBI agents from outside jurisdictions came to interview Randall and Steph. They used our home for interviews at the request of Randall and Steph. Other witnesses, all meth users, were also contacted and interviewed by the FBI over the course of the day. Toward the end of the day the FBI agents advised they would be in contact with us and thanked us for the assistance. Steph and Randall departed with the agents, leaving us with hopes that our lives would return to some degree of normalcy.

After several days the agents informed me they had turned over all their information to the Kalispell Police Department and that they would be handling the local interviews and investigation. They stated they were going to pursue information of crimes outside of the Flathead Valley and gave me the names of Kalispell Police Investigators who would be contacting us for further information and interviews.

Mr Dower was arrested several months later for multiple crimes involving prostitution, conspiracy, sexual conduct with minors, etc. Randall was advised he had violated his parole and that a parole violation hearing would be held in a few weeks. Randall had admitted he was providing meth and other drugs to the girls involved with Mr Dower in return for money, but denied using drugs himself; that proved to be false. Randall had relapsed and again was using meth. Steph had not used, but lost custody of her children due to her activities with Mr Dower and was arrested and convicted for prostitution along with several other young women who were involved with Dower.

Teens in Crisis members considered the investigation all but over and we all moved on with our lives. Regardless of my attempts to bring my family activities back to some degree of normalcy, Carren became apprehensive about all the arrests and constantly questioned me about whether our family was safe due to my personal involvement in the investigation.

I told her we had always had to be careful since her days of using drugs and used my standard metaphor: 'If you crawl into the sewer you're bound to come out smelling like shit and chances are you're going to get some of it on the people you are close to.'

She laughed and agreed not to worry.

I didn't believe we were completely safe, but there was no reason to create alarm without cause. Carren chose to live at home after graduating her rehab program and we were both attending the local community college. Carren challenged me to attend college with her and bet me she could get a better grade point average. We were in a fierce competition for grades for over two years. Carren for the first time was interested in school and I didn't want her to have any distractions. She had pulled straight A's for the past year and was proud of her personal success. I checked with the local police and was advised to be careful and just watch for anything out of the ordinary, but beyond that to just live life as normally as possible.

A week or so later I was parking my truck at the local golf course. I was planning on playing just nine holes of golf and then heading off to an appointment with a crisis family. John, a friend from group, had just pulled up beside me and was planning on giving me a ride to the club house. As I was getting out of my car I heard a voice from behind me yelling, 'Turn around I want to talk to you.'

It was Randall; he was walking up to me briskly with a scowl on his face, furrowed brows and appeared angry. He immediately started yelling, 'You ruined my life, you fucking asshole. I have been talking to Dale Dower and now we will see how you like someone coming after your family.'

I stepped toward Randall, clenching my fist and challenged him. 'Are you threatening my family, you dirt bag?'

He stepped back and repeated his statement. 'Let's see how you like someone coming after you and your family, you asshole.' He then immediately turned away and walked down the street.

I turned to John and asked if he had heard what Randall had just said and he nodded.

'John, I need to call the police right away.'

John agreed. I immediately called Kalispell Police Department and they asked if I would come in later in the afternoon and complete a statement. I agreed and set the appointment for 3:00 pm that afternoon. After making a report I went home, trying to decide how to tell my family that we were evidently not safe. Next I had to decide the best way to protect my family. The police stated they would provide extra patrol for our home and they would pass the information about Randall to his parole officer. They advised me to be careful and call again if I observed any suspicious activity.

When I got home I checked the phone for messages and was shocked to hear Dale Dower's voice leaving a message asking me to call him. I had not talked to him in over a year. He had been in jail, had bailed out and was awaiting trial. He knew I had called in the FBI, had worked with the local police, and had encouraged parents and their children to cooperate with the authorities. Now what? Did he plan on getting me off somewhere and offering me a bribe to help stop the investigation, or maybe he was angry enough to harm me.

I called the police and told them the circumstances and asked what they wanted me to do. They told me they wanted to discuss the situation with the county attorney and other investigators. In a few minutes they called me back and asked if I would be willing to meet with Mr Dower and take a hidden recording device. I replied that I would be willing to meet with Dower and agreed to recording the meeting in case anything went wrong and someone ended up getting hurt. The meeting was set up for the following Friday. I just had to wait and figure out what to tell my family.

I asked Karyl, Carren and Scott to all be at home that evening for a family meeting. I told them of the events of the day; about Randall threatening the family and about the upcoming meeting with Dale Dower. Karyl was visibly shaken, Carren asked if there was reason to be frightened and Scott said, 'Go meet with him Dad and ask him why he sent that dirt bag to threaten you.'

I told them that the police advised us to be careful and not to go places alone:

'Just be vigilant in watching your surroundings.' I told them the police were going to provide extra patrol at our home and that they need not be alarmed if they saw lights flashing on the house at night. After we had discussed all the possibilities and concerns we decided to let it rest till morning and discuss it again later.

The next morning started off just like a typical day. Everyone in a rush to get dressed, breakfast, cars loaded up, and off to school, work and whatever. As far as I could tell, there didn't appear to be any emotional after effects from the information I shared the night before. Carren asked if she could talk to me later in the day after classes and I told her when I would be home. She seemed calm and relaxed, yet I could sense something was bothering her.

I have to admit I was wondering if there was a chance she had had any contact with Dower when she was living on the streets. There had been so many girls involved with Dower and all were involved with meth; could one of them have been Carren?

Carren and I met later that afternoon and she advised me she wanted to move out of the Flathead Valley. She just couldn't live with all the stress of being threatened, the publicity created by the Dower case, and the ridicule from Dower supporters at our church. She said she was going to take a job in Yellowstone National Park for the summer and would decide what to do about school in the fall. I told her I didn't think there was anything to be afraid of, but I wasn't very convincing with my argument. Carren said she had made up her mind to go. She reaffirmed that she was clean and sober and there was not a problem with drugs or alcohol, she just needed to start a life without all the drama created by meth here in our community.

I had to admit our lives were chaotic due to our involvement with Teens in Crisis and all the families with kids in crisis. I told her I supported her decision and gave her a hug. I asked, 'How soon will you be leaving'?

'As soon as I finish my last class this semester,' she replied.

I also asked if Carren knew how Scott was taking this entire Dower thing. She replied that Scott wasn't afraid or anything, but that he was thinking of going into the Marines and felt the sooner the better. She reached out and gave me a hug and reassured me I had done the right thing.

'Dad, I love you, thank you for honoring your commitment to me. Everything will be OK.'

A few weeks after Carren moved to Yellowstone, I received the following letter from her.

Hi Dad,

I am in Yellowstone National Park and I will be living in a little majestic town called Mammoth Hot Springs. Mammoth is located just inside the park when you come in from Gardner, Mt. I am officially a wrangler as I write this letter. I can't believe they are actually going to pay me to ride horses in this quaint little place. Our job will be taking families on vacation on horseback rides throughout the mountains surrounding Mammoth Hot Springs, the most beautiful place in the world. I am glad I am here and I hope you understand.

I am sorry to have left home so quickly. I know that you had great hopes for me in college and I agree this will set me back a bit as far as my education is concerned, but in my heart I know I needed to leave for me. I believe the job at Yellowstone Park was God's way of helping me to keep my sanity. Things at home were becoming overwhelming for me. You kept your promise about helping my friends and I support all you have done over the last few years at Teens in Crisis. Yet regardless of where I go or who I see, someone wants to talk to me about Meth, kids on drugs, the dangers about suicide, or some other terrible crisis. I feel as though every time I turn around someone is asking me to relive those horrible five months I lived for Meth. Constantly reliving the events makes it seem as if there is a ghost attempting to lure me back to the places I don't want to go. Dad, I don't ever want to be that person again and right now all of the drama and chaos is taking its toll.

Meth is everywhere and to be honest these past few months have been truly unbearable. I respect your efforts, our efforts, to help parents and their children, but I am not sure you realize the danger this has created for our family; threatening phone calls, police checking up on us, and your repeated warnings to be on the alert. I don't feel as if I can go get a cup of coffee or go to dinner with friends without being on my guard. I am constantly watching for druggies that you or members of your group have turned into the police. The most terrifying thing for me is that there is always someone I recognize but I can't remember from where.

Once again I find myself being terrified of the dark that night brings. I used to feel peace and enjoyment and appreciation for the silence. Now I am fearful and I keep remembering the never ending nights and days when I lived on the streets. Often when I lay in bed and close my eyes I feel like someone dark and sinister is standing over me. Driving home from work at night, I find myself checking headlights in my rear view mirror and I am afraid that someone is following me. I find myself driving home different ways each night hoping I will be able to recognize if someone is following me.

The Dale Dower thing ultimately has me spinning. The feeling that I cannot trust the friends we once believed in is maddening. I find myself questioning the friendship of people that have been lifelong friends; fear and regret is filling my heart and I hate this way of living. At church I get the feeling people think we are to blame for Dale Dower's action and they are mad at us for what I believe was doing the right thing. I am being judged even though I still don't understand all that is involved. Is our church a safe place for us? I just don't know.

Steph and Randall have been my heroes throughout my recovery since coming home and to learn that they are part of this scandal makes me fearful of my own success. When the FBI came to our house and you sent us to get the other witnesses they told me that you didn't know the extent that you have involved yourself and your family. They said 'no one is as they seem' and we are all in danger.

Everyone that I have relied on for support and hope has relapsed or are involved in some kind of scandal. You know the statistics and I don't want to be one of the nine out of ten people who aren't going to beat this. Even after three years the temptation to use is still in my thoughts and I feel that we have worked too hard, too long, and come too far; I am not willing to jeopardize our success. I know that you understand what I am telling you because I have watched you struggle as well: If people have to ask why I left, they don't deserve to know.

The odds are against me in the Flathead Valley and despite my fear of leaving you, mom, and Scott, I have to go. For the love of myself and my family I am making this choice. I love you and will miss you. Please do not stop praying for me, I will need it more now than ever. Thank you for the second chance and I offer these words that I keep close to my heart:

Amazing Grace, how sweet the sound,
That saved a wretch like me . . .
I once was lost but now am found,
Was blind, but now, I see.

T'was Grace that taught my heart to fear.
And Grace, my fears relieved.
How precious did that Grace appear . . .
The hour I first believed.

Through many dangers, toils and snares . . .
We have already come.
T'was Grace that brought us safe thus far . . .
And Grace will lead us home.

The Lord has promised good to me . . .
His word my hope secures.
He will my shield and portion be . . .
As long as life endures.

When we've been here ten thousand years . . .
Bright shining as the sun.
We've no less days to sing God's praise . . .
Then when we've first begun.

Amazing Grace, how sweet the sound,
That saved a wretch like me . . .
I once was lost but now am found,
Was blind, but now, I see.

All my love,
Carren

The morning I was to meet with Dale Dower, Karyl pleaded with me not to go.

'It is none of your business Ron; just let the police handle it.'

'Karyl, our family has been threatened and our children are leaving home as a direct result of that threat. I am not going to run away from Dower or anyone else that has threatened our family or is involved with meth. I am going to meet with him and find out what he wants! The police will be standing by if I need anything.'

Karyl started to cry and said, 'Fine, you never listen to anyone,' and she walked out the door.

The meeting was to take place at Dower's now-empty home located west of Kalispell. Prior to the meeting I was told to come to the police station and was given a digital recorder which I was to just turn on before entering his home to record the meeting. I was introduced to the two officers who would be parked nearby in case I needed help for any reason.

I met with Dale Dower along with his wife for over two hours. Information from that meeting identified other participants involved in the Dower prostitution ring. He was prosecuted, convicted and sent to prison. Randall was sent back to the state prison in Deer Lodge, Montana for violating his parole. Several of the girls involved with Dower were convicted of prostitution. Maybe now our life would get back to normal, then again maybe not.

Although meth wasn't being used in our home, the effects were again causing our family to split up: Carren moving to Yellowstone and Scott signing up for the Marines. I was thankful Alicia was living in Bozeman, yet the effects of the investigation and my name surfaced in her local newspaper. I immediately got a call as soon as Alicia saw the paper.

'Dad, what is going on at home? Are you guys safe? It is all over the papers here about you meeting with Dale Dower and taping the conversation.'

I explained to her briefly the details and how it all came about. Alicia wanted to know if she was safe even though she was living in Bozeman, Mt.

My reply was simple. 'You are as safe as anyone can be, Alicia. Don't worry and have fun in school.'

There was no doubt it was time to have Carren and Scott leave the Flathead Valley and quite possibly time for us to start over somewhere else as well.

Regardless of our efforts, meth is still being used by kids. Stealing, dealing and screwing were still the methods of acquiring money and drugs. Carren had moved away and Scott was a Marine. Now all I had to do was figure out how to heal the hurt between Karyl and me, and learn to live a life, once again, without our children.

EPILOGUE

*I looked around our church, about five years ago, and I saw kids
disappearing. You could see kids who were troubled and then, poof, they
were gone.*

Ron Clem

Carren and I have chosen to share our lives, in hopes that students, parents, grandparents, extended families, teachers, and community leaders will understand drug abuse can happen to anyone. The fact is: hurting kids make poor choices. We hope and pray that our book in some small way will prevent another child from taking the painful journey of addiction, prostitution, or criminal behavior.

We have dedicated this book to the families that have lost their children due to drug abuse. Throughout Montana and the United States children are dying and families are suffering the loss due to drug and alcohol abuse by their children. We feel it is important to share with you the events that led to the deaths of the children of those families to whom we have dedicated our book. Each family has hopes that through their loss others will take the necessary steps to save their children and prevent what each family has to live with daily: the loss of their child.

THE FAMILIES

Steve and Susan Stapley

Leslie Ann Stapley Kirkland   December 21st, 1971 to May 4th, 2000

Leslie Ann Stapley Kirkland, age 28, went to be with her Lord and Creator Thursday May 4th, 2000. She was born in American Falls, Idaho, December 21st, 1971, to Steve and Shirley Ann Stapley. She moved to the Columbia Falls area as a small child with her parents. She attended school in Columbia Falls, graduating in 1990.

She was preceded in death by her husband, Tim Kirkland.

She is survived by her two children, Jacquelyn and Christian; her parents, Steve and Susan Stapley and Shirley Ann Gurley of Seattle; three brothers, grandparents, and numerous aunts, uncles, cousins, and many precious and dear friends.

She will be greatly missed by all.

Leslie Ann, mother of two beautiful children, and sister to three brothers, died by suicide battling her meth addiction. The parents Steve and Susan are raising their grandchildren the best they can; however, they admit the grandchildren need their mother. Steve and Susan wish their daughter would had made a different choice, a choice to see her children grow and have children of their own.

'Suicide is a permanent solution to a temporary problem. We miss our daughter everyday, but we cannot even imagine the lasting impact it will have on the children throughout their lives.'

Let not mercy and truth forsake you; bind them around your neck, write them on the tablet of your heart ... Trust in the Lord with all your heart, and lean not on your own understanding. In all your ways acknowledge Him, and he shall direct your paths.

Proverbs 3: 3, 5–6

Troy and Gerri Gardner

Anji Gardner   December 31st, 1980 to November 27th, 2000

Anji Gardner was introduced to drugs by her employer at a local fast food restaurant in Whitefish, Montana. Gerri has often said, 'It was her choice to use, but it was our choice not to take action to stop her drug abuse.'

Anji ended up with several felony arrests centering on her attempts to steal enough money to buy the meth she so desperately needed. After being convicted and sentenced to the Department of Corrections, Anji gave up on life and ran from the Connections Correction facility where she was being housed. She committed suicide a few days later, unable to live a life without meth, yet wishing everyday she had never used that very first time.

Gerri's husband never forgave himself for not protecting his daughter from her drug of choice. He blamed her death on his failure as a father. He committed suicide sixteen months after Anji's death.

Gerri continues to work with families, schools, and Teens in Crisis assisting other parents with kids in crisis.

Connie Guzman

Angela Guzman   *June 8th, 1978 to October 13th, 2003*

Connie Guzman's daughter Angi died in a fiery car accident. Both the driver and Angi were under the influence of meth at the time of the accident. Angi had been battling her meth addiction for over three years with no success. Angi had three children. Connie adores her grandchildren but admits they all miss their mom desperately every day.

News release by Hal Hearing, *New West Magazine*, 3-17-05

In the days since Angela Guzman-Rogers' friend Ryan had been released from the Flathead County Jail, they'd celebrated his new freedom by keeping the Methamphetamine buzz at fever pitch. Nothing really compares to that first shot of Crystal Meth when you're just out of jail – but like everything good, that rush is impossible to hold on to. After a couple of days of mainlining, the rush isn't coming back, and at four in the morning on the third day you're scraping the bottom of your bag with a razor so hard that the plastic comes curling away with the last residue of the dope.

Angela and Ryan were ready to get out of Kalispell. Between them and two friends they were holding $5,000, and Angela had her mother's car, a reliable red Subaru Legacy. They all got high again and headed for Colville, Washington, to meet a cooker and get some more dope. An identified young man rode with Angela into the cold predawn of October 13th, 2003. Ryan rode in the lead car, to show them all which way to go.

The road west is Highway 2, which leaves the Flathead Valley and winds through an endless dark timber county of low mountains and thicketed river bottoms. But Angela would never get to see that road again. The lead car sailed through the flashing red light at the intersection of Highway 2 and Reserve Street, still in Kalispell, and Angela followed without a pause. A massive self-loading logging truck headed out for the first run of the day slammed into the driver's side of the Subaru at an estimated 45 miles per hour.

Angela was killed instantly, thrown, still hanging in her seatbelt, into the passenger side of the car. For her passenger it must have been like being inside a detonating bomb, but he survived. He staggered from the wreck, bleeding from a head wound, and staggered into the dawn.

Greg and Mary Haydal

Cassie Haydal   *August 14th, 1982 to November 14th, 2000*

Greg and Mary Haydal, Dale City ranchers, had the life so many of us dream of: two beautiful children, Cassie and Nicole, horses, dogs, cats, grandparents living nearby. They were living life to the fullest in the Last Best Place. Neither Greg nor Mary had any idea their oldest daughter had ever used drugs and never in their wildest dreams would they have believed she had been using meth for over a year. She was an A student in school, destined for college the following year, an athlete; the model child. Yet suddenly one afternoon their daughter collapsed after coaching her sister's basketball team. The diagnosis was massive heart failure due to methamphetamine abuse. Cassie's death stunned the quaint little community of Dale City. How could something like this happen here?

News release: Waging War on Drugs – Bob Feist, *News Argus*

In November of 2000 the world darkened for a Dale City family when 18-year-old Cassie Haydal died due to methamphetamine use. Cassie's mom, Mary Haydal, shared her story with the community of Lewistown last week in a series of presentations.

During her talks, Haydal told her story of heartbreak, anger and struggling with decisions while watching her daughter dying in a coma. 'I kept asking myself: Where did I go wrong as a mother?'

Cassie collapsed on the floor of the bathroom at her country home in Dale City after coaching her sister's basketball practice. Her mother struggled to resuscitate her as her sister drove to a neighbor's house to get help. After arriving at the hospital in Dale City, shock treatments finally revived Cassie. But that was when the family received the sad news that Cassie's body was filled with Methamphetamines.

News spread fast through the community and soon several of Cassie's friends and classmates were at the hospital. 'Everyone was crying and apologizing,' said Haydal. 'You see drugs don't just affect the user.' When our kids make choices about drugs and alcohol, it affects everyone around them.

She learned from Cassie's friends that her daughter had been using Meth for more than a year. Cassie's friends were apologizing for not telling the family.

'How do you tell if your child is doing okay?' Haydal asked the parents. The responses included having friends, getting good grades, and going to church. All of these things fit Cassie's profile. Cassie was an honor student who went to church with her family. She volunteered for after school programs, was always happy and had lots of friends.

The family had noticed changes in Cassie before her collapse but figured they were normal teen things. They had taken her to the doctor to check on a persistent cough. 'Just like everyone else, doctor's stereotype,' said Haydal. 'They never thought Cassie would be using drugs, so they didn't test for them.'

Dan, Linda and Angela Smith

Heather Ann Smith   *October 17th, 1980 to August 10th, 1999*

Heather Ann Smith, 18, died Tuesday, August 10th, 1999. Her organs were donated Wednesday, August 11th, 1999, to Life Center Northwest Donor Network through Kalispell Regional Medical Center.

She attended school at Montessori, Fairmont-Egan, Kalispell Junior High, and graduated from Flathead High School in 1998. She was pursuing her dream of becoming a registered nurse through Flathead Valley Community College and the Montana University System.

She was baptized Lutheran and is being mourned by a multitude of friends and family as a result of this most unfortunate death.

She is survived by her parents, Dr R.D. Smith and wife, Linda Elaine, and sister Angela Danielle Smith, all of Kalispell . . .

The family suggests memorials be sent in honor of Heather A. Smith to Flathead Valley Community College Nursing Scholarship Fund.

Dan and Linda lived on a small ranch east of Kalispell, Montana: Two beautiful children, Heather and Angie. They believed life couldn't get any better. At age seventeen and a half Heather came home and advised her mother and father she was in love with a boy and they were going to live together. Shocked and in disbelief, they attempted to discourage their daughter's decision. The effort was futile: Heather soon moved from their home and began a life with her new boyfriend. Dan and Linda were beside themselves with concern for Heather's well-being. How could their daughter make such a choice in direct conflict with their family values? Heather continued to maintain family contact even though Dan and Linda constantly reaffirmed their dissatisfaction with Heather's choice.

They soon learned from Heather that her new boyfriend was using drugs on a regular basis. Regardless of Heather's efforts she was unable to discourage her boyfriend to quit his drug use. Heather originally felt she could change her boyfriend's lifestyle and choice to abuse drugs and alcohol but she quickly learned her efforts were useless. After several months, Heather decided to move out and continue to pursue her dreams of becoming a registered nurse. She had just received her acceptance into the nursing program at Montana State University, Bozeman, and proudly boasted about her new dreams in life to her mom and dad.

As Heather often said, her boyfriend was constantly under the influence and she couldn't live her life like that any longer. Heather revealed that her boyfriend was continuing to use drugs and now was failing to answer calls for work. The more Heather challenged her boyfriend about his behavior the more physically abusive he became. Heather's friends finally warned Dan and Linda that Heather was suffering significant physical abuse from her boyfriend and that they needed to take action immediately. Heather finally made the decision to leave the relationship which incensed her boyfriend. It was then that he made the decision that would change the Smith family forever: He declared he would never allow her to leave him and shot her in the head killing her instantly.

He ended up serving four plus years with the Department of Corrections in Deer Lodge, Montana and the Smith family received the sentence: life without their daughter and beloved sister. Her boyfriend has never taken responsibility for Heather's death or expressed remorse for his crime. The trauma of Heather's death continues to plague Dan and Linda daily; and the loss of her older sister has left Angie with emptiness that has yet to be filled.

The Jorgenson Family

Helena, Montana

They don't know when their daughter began using meth. She had used alcohol on occasions and began changing friends and behaviors. She was their little girl and they believed nothing would ever change that. Then meth entered their daughter's world. Meth became their daughter's only focus in life and soon having her gone wherever was easier than her being home.

Another night spent with her new best friend meth was all she cared about. A little more alcohol, another hit of meth. She wasn't sure if it was bad stuff or if she was just strung out beyond belief. She knew she wanted to get home. There was the door, Mom and Dad inside, it was so cold outside; winters were like that in Montana.

No one knows if she ever knocked on the door. The next morning her parents found her cold lifeless body lying in the front yard. Meth had taken another child.

CARREN

Carren has been clean and sober for five years. She will always be a meth addict. It is her choice whether she will be in recovery or not. There have been no relapses, but again there are no guarantees. As parents we had to realize that we either support her in her efforts at sobriety or assist her addiction. There is no middle ground.

Recently Carren shared her thoughts about her recovery, about her life, and hopes for her future. Her words say it best:

'It has been five years now since I left the streets of the Flathead Valley. As tranquil and safe as the valley appears, to me it will always hold dark secrets. To return even for short visits gives me a sense of foreboding; an uneasiness. Each and every day is a battle to stay clean, some days are better than others; returning home makes those days worse. Throughout my recovery, be it in the program at Tranquility Bay or back in the real world learning to live a "normal" life, I am constantly reminded of things that I have been told: Avoid old non-working friends, keep positive, don't use any substance that might jeopardize your recovery, be honest with yourself, and pick friends that will support your sobriety. I have constant questions and challenges but to stay sober I find myself always going back to the techniques and tools taught me during my recovery program.

'I start each day with my declaration of who I am: "I am a forgiven, beautiful, confident, magical child of God." Then I ask myself, "Is it all worth it?" I answer boldly out loud, "Yes every minute of every day." I wake up in the morning and I choose to be happy. I look at where I am living and know my life is working for me. I have made choices that have jeopardized my sobriety, but because I surround myself with friends who realize how important sobriety is to me, they challenge me to make choices that will keep my life on track. I don't always know what I need to do or change, but I know the concept "It takes a community to raise a child" holds true for those of us in recovery.

'The Twelve Step Program was introduced to me in Jamaica and continues to be a source of strength for me on a daily basis. One key point that has helped me more than others is to yield to a higher power. I was raised a Christian and throughout the years I have fought my faith. I blamed God for my choices. I wanted nothing to do with some all knowing being that allowed me to be raped and repeatedly hurt over the years. There were days when I didn't think I could take another consequence when in treatment, or couldn't see how to get another homework assignment done, complete another day of work at a job I desperately hated, or deal with the intense emotional ups and downs of the relationships in my life. I needed to be able to turn everything over to something larger, something grander than myself. I finally realized I needed to live my life for something greater than myself and I wouldn't have made it in treatment or in my life today without my higher power.

'I now get high by hiking to towering peaks and quiet valleys. The beauty all around me makes me realize how wonderful life really is. My values and standards are appreciated by my friends who live by those same values and standards. I love life and the gift of beauty God has created here in Yellowstone. I have been given a second chance and I never want to take that for granted.

'I live each day one day at a time and I can say that I am thankful I am alive.'

Letter from Carren in Yellowstone National Park, June 12th, 2004

Hi Dad,

I am off today and preparing to go on a hike with some friends. I have learned to love the beauty of the outdoors and especially the mountains. I don't know if I ever shared with you the contribution Alicia made towards my sobriety. When she came home just before I left for Yellowstone she asked if I would like to go for a hike in Glacier National Park. Of course you know I rarely participated in any of that type of activities since, since, well for a long time. Anyway, Alicia said we were going to climb a mountain. My reply was, are you sure you want me to go along? Alicia said yes I am sure; I can't give you much to help you with your life, but I can share what makes me happy and that is being in the mountains.

Being home wasn't as easy as I thought it was going to be. I had worked so hard so I could be back here sleeping in my own bed and be with my family and yet I still was missing something. I didn't have any friends because they were either in jail, dead or still using drugs. I wasn't socially active because I couldn't find friends that weren't using drugs or alcohol: Thus I focused on school and being active with Teens in Crisis. Essentially, I was lonely even though I had you and Mom.

When Alicia asked me to join her in Glacier Park it came at the right time and just at the right moment. It had been some time since we had seen each other. Anyway it sounded like fun and I agreed to do it. It would be nice to go and do something away from the house. The drive up was beautiful as always; the 'Going to the Sun' highway was absolutely spectacular. I can't say I enjoyed the ride up, perched on the edge of the road looking down 5000 feet to the valley below. Yet the thrill and my typical reaction of hugging the center console made Alicia and I both laugh. Being in Jamaica I had forgotten how dramatic the changes in elevation are when driving in real mountains. Before too long we were parking at the trail head, preparing for the eight mile round trip hike. I was excited. The hike was fairly moderate; however, due to the altitude I could feel the shortage in oxygen. Alicia didn't appear to have any trouble with the climb. There was not a lot of conversation between us as we climbed and that was OK; the experience alone was enough. Growing up we never really hung out or did things like this and the fact that after all the hurt and bitterness over the last couple of years I was glad we were doing something together. Nothing else in the world mattered.

We continued to hike and take unbelievable pictures. At one point we looked up and to our left there was a good sized moose. As we climbed higher the wind accelerated and the temperature dropped. It became quite apparent I hadn't dressed for the occasion. I was so cold and with the steepest climb ahead of us, I made the decision to stop. Alicia wanted to keep going and I told her I would wait for her in the shelter of a rock enclave bordering the trail. She went ahead and climbed to the top and I waited for her as agreed. I used the time to absorb all of the beauty around me. It was as though I was standing on the top of the world. There were miles and miles of jagged mountains spread out before me. For the first time in years I felt a familiar feeling, the exhilaration was unbelievable, better than ever before, yet Meth wasn't involved: The high was just as intense if not more. I loved where we were and what we had achieved. I felt as though I could achieve anything in the world; once again 'I was superwoman.' The hike back down was silent and steady. We were both ready to get back to the car and the wonderful invention of car heaters. On the drive home I decided it was okay that I didn't have an abundance of friends and I appreciated that I had my family.

Dad, I know what I have to do to keep sober. Enjoy life everyday. It may not always be thrilling as climbing a mountain, but I have to admit I am glad I am alive with God's beauty all around me.

If life gets too stressful, my advice is go climb a mountain. God is up there just waiting to show you what he has created.

Love Carren

Karyl and I are still in the process of putting our family back together. There has been so much hurt experienced by all of us.

Alicia just can't understand why Carren made such stupid choices. 'Didn't Carren know how much it hurt all of us?'

Scott couldn't deal with all the pain at home, the ridicule from friends, and the chaos in our community: He joined the Marines to start a new life.

Karyl and I are actively involved in Teens in Crisis, a family support group for parents in similar situations. We pray Carren remains clean and sober. We have expended all of our resources on Carren's recovery and have nothing left if she relapses.

There are no guarantees, but we believe that God gave us this child and it was our responsibility to give her a chance to live again.

I am glad to say that Stephen was arrested for possession of dangerous drugs, possession for sale, and distribution. He is currently serving time in Federal Prison for drug-related crimes.

Collette was last heard from in the spring of 2004; she was living on the streets in Seattle, still using drugs, supporting her habit any way she could.

Red was arrested by the Northwest Drug Task Force for possession of dangerous drugs, possession for sales, and distribution of dangerous drugs. His trailer burned down under suspicious circumstances.

Jerry, the dealer from the canyon was arrested by the Northwest Drug Task Force for possession of dangerous drugs, possession for sales, and distribution. He is currently serving time in state prison, Deer Lodge, Montana.

Crazy George is still on the streets as far as anyone knows. He hasn't quite been himself for some time now.

'Skids' has left the area and hasn't been seen for several years. I can only hope he finally found someone that could return the brutality he relished inflicting on others.

APPENDIX A   THE DAILY INTER LAKE

The irony is that Ron Clem moved his family to Montana to escape the dark influences that might threaten his children in California.

Chery Sabol, Daily Inter Lake

Daily Inter Lake, Chery Sabol, June 2001

Retired from the Los Angeles Police Department, Clem finds those forces are as potent in Whitefish as in Watts

He sadly admits now that his 18-year-old daughter 'is a druggie,' addicted to methamphetamine she discovered in the Flathead Valley.

'I'm not comfortable,' talking about the decline of my daughter, Carren, into a life defined by drugs, sex, and thefts to support her habit, he said.

But he's compelled to tell others, as a kind of parental parable that could spare them the pain that overtakes him mid-sentence and makes him grieve for his daughter's innocence. Carren is safely at a treatment facility in Jamaica now, in a program that has facilities nationwide, as close as Thompson Falls. That she's alive to suffer through the predictable depression and cravings of a four-month withdrawal is astounding enough. 'She tried to kill herself,' Clem said. 'She finally got strung out to an unbelievable point.'

He and his wife 'had kind of already started our mourning,' of the daughter who once played violin and rode horses.

It was about a year ago that 'I noticed her getting high,' he said. Carren was going to college and working full-time after obtaining her high-school equivalent degree. She began drinking and smoking marijuana while at Whitefish High School, she's told her parents.

Her first experience with methamphetamine, as a way to 'boost' her through days after nights of partying, addicted her, Clem said.

He and his wife had no way of knowing what Carren was doing, but they wouldn't tolerate her coming home high.

'We put the screws on and she bailed out,' he said.

Helpless, knowing his girl was drifting through homes in Whitefish; he contacted family court services, probation officers, and anyone he could think of. He shadowed Carren as she went to unsupervised homes where he suspects drugs were sold and homes where parents turned their heads to teens' drug activities. 'It's absolutely unbelievable. It's happening to our kids,' he said. 'Parents knew these kids were doing all this.'

Clem knew his daughter was in serious trouble. It hit home when he read a newspaper story about Gerri Gardner, whose daughter, also from Whitefish, gave up on her battle with addiction by killing herself.

'We began panicking after your articles. Death was not an option,' Carren's parents decided. 'If we can get her to get her life back, and then her self esteem . . . then it's up to her. We can forget all the activities that brought us to this point. We love her so much,' Clem said. But those activities still break his heart. In a letter nearly 40 pages long, Carren confessed to her parents the kind of lifestyle she'd fallen into. It is impossible to read without flinching at the thought of a loving father consuming the words.

In another letter, she wrote more generally about her despair.

'I was tired. It seemed the more money I spent on drugs, the more it took and I still didn't have the energy I needed to make it through each day. It was horrible waking up in the morning and not knowing what I did the night before and knowing that I had traded a wonderful life with you guys for a life as a dirt bag,' Carren wrote.

It was a lifestyle Clem couldn't reconcile with what he had always wanted for her, Clem said. 'You always dream of your little girls getting married and having a family and grandkids, having a job and being successful. When that's gone, then you just hope for life and a chance to start over. That's where we're at,' he said. The program is no quick fix. 'Treatment can last as long as two years,' Clem said. And it doesn't come cheap. Because of that, some residents are building a scholarship program for other teens that need treatment. In this area, donors can contact Clem at TeensnCrisis.org on the Internet.

There's no guarantee for Carren's recovery. But there's no prayer for it if she's not in treatment, her parents decided. And it's not just their daughter at stake. The family has lived in the valley for 21 years and the changes swirling around teens have astounded them, Clem said.

'I looked around our church, about five years ago, and I saw kids disappearing. You could see kids who were troubled and then, poof, they were gone,' he said. He's convinced many fell victim to methamphetamine, the vilest of drugs the retired cop knows. 'A good, clean heroin addict is ten times better,' than a meth addict, he said. And so he tells Carren's story, in hopes that it will help, in hopes that 'I never have to look in a man's eyes and see the loss and hollowness' that comes with being the parent of an addict. 'Maybe parents will watch their kids and see changes in their personality before it's too late,' he said. Maybe they can watch for unusual traffic in their neighborhoods. Maybe they'll be alert to the money that comes and goes through their teens' hands. Addicts are clever in concealing their habits, but 'We don't have to make it easy for them,' he said.

'We as parents have to be accountable. I think this community's strong enough to tackle it. It's impacting us all. You've got to be bold and be courageous. You've got to step out and take action or you're going to lose these kids.

'If you value your children's lives, don't be timid,' Clem said.

APPENDIX B   METHAMPHETAMINE

Common and brand names
Go Fast, Meth; Speed; Crystal; Glass; Crank; Tweak, Yaba;
Desoxyn, Ice

Effects classification
Euphoric Stimulant

Chemical name
d-N-methyl amphetamine

Description
Methamphetamine is a strong physical and mental stimulant in
both prescription and street forms. It is relatively easy to
synthesize which has contributed to its widespread use. Erowid
Vault, 2006

Methamphetamine is increasingly available throughout the United
States and is becoming more popular in the UK and other European
countries. Results from recent surveys indicated that meth is a
growing problem throughout rural America and is quickly spread-
ing throughout cities in the East Coast (*Meth in the City*, A&E

Special television presentation). Law enforcement officers across the country identify methamphetamine as the most significant drug problem in their jurisdictions. Emergency services and first responders have reported a significant increase in methamphetamine-related treatment episodes and calls for service. The majority of methamphetamine being distributed is trafficked by Mexican national groups. Additionally, numerous small-scale local laboratory operators, producing up to ounce quantities of methamphetamine for personal use and/or local distribution are still producing product in states that have not enacted controls on psuedo-ephedrine. These mom and pop labs continue to create significant environmental hazards in the communities where meth is manufactured.

At the Siebel Scholarship Conference recently held in Chicago, Philanthropist Tom Siebel dedicated the conference to finding solutions for the growing problem of Methamphetamine use in America. Experts in the field of prevention, treatment and enforcement agreed that Methamphetamine users are difficult to survey. The onset of severe paranoia due to continued use of Meth creates hesitancy by the abuser to respond to standard survey techniques. The consensus by many participating experts warned against information suggesting a reduction in Meth use by teens and young adults without supporting data from emergency treatment facilities, first responders, child protective services, short-term detention facilities, and criminal courts. Recent surveys conducted by the Siebel funded Montana Meth Project revealed startling information. Despite prevention and education efforts by local, state and private agencies, 65% of teens, 12–17 years of age, reported Meth readily available. 33% reported being offered Meth within the last year, and 27% had no perceived risk of using Meth.

Recent Town Hall meetings held in Washington D.C. hosted by senators Max Baucus, Montana, Norm Coleman, Minnesota, and Conrad Burns, Montana, characterized current Meth use in America as pandemic. US Attorney General Alberto Gonzales introduced his observations on Meth stating: 'The scourge of methamphetamine is tightening its grip on communities across America. As we have heard, meth is a unique and deadly threat to our Nation. It is highly addictive. It is easy and cheap to produce. And as many in this room know, it destroys lives far beyond those of just the addicts and the users.

'With every tragedy and every act of violence . . . with every child abandoned because of meth use and every life lost to meth abuse

... the vise grip is turned another notch. And that means community and national leaders are being squeezed for answers – for some response to this rapidly growing problem.'

The Meth crisis facing our families and communities will only be stopped when we, as a nation, make the decision to implement decisive prevention programs, such as the Not Even Once Campaign being funded by the Montana Meth Project. Additionally effective verifiable treatment programs must be made available to Meth users. And finally, aggressive interdiction and arrest procedures must be implemented and funded in efforts to reduce the availability of Meth.

Meth has been characterized as the one drug of abuse that has the ability to alter the American social and economic infrastructure. The long term effects on families, local economies, and our greatest national treasure, our children, is taking a horrific toll. To voice the state wide campaign initiated by Tom Siebel, founder of the Montana Meth Project, with Meth – 'Not even Once!'

UK USE OF METH

'A new highly addictive drug used in Britain by clubbers and gay men is becoming a global problem,' according to a United Nations report published March of 2006. This was the similar pattern of Meth use along the Eastern seaboard of the US until the drug was discovered by teen and young adult users.

'It has not affected that much of Western European countries and the UK but, as we know, as drug misuse occurs in North America, sooner of later it gets here [Europe]' (Professor Hamid Ghodse, United Nations Drug Control Agency)

APPENDIX C BEHAVIOR CHARACTERISTICS ASSOCIATED WITH SUBSTANCE ABUSE

In large doses, methamphetamine's frequent effects are irritability, aggressive behavior, anxiety, excitement, auditory hallucinations, and paranoia (delusions and psychosis). **Abusers tend to be violent.** Mood changes are common, and the abuser can rapidly change from friendly to hostile. The paranoia produced by methamphetamine use results in suspiciousness, hyperactive behavior, and dramatic mood swings.

- Abrupt changes in work or school attendance, quality of work, work output, grades, discipline.
- Unusual flare-ups or outbreaks of temper.
- Withdrawal from responsibility.
- General changes in overall attitude.
- Deterioration of physical appearance and grooming.
- Wearing of sunglasses at inappropriate times.
- Continual wearing of long-sleeved garments particularly in hot weather or reluctance to wear short-sleeved attire when appropriate.

- Association with known substance abusers.
- Unusual borrowing of money from friends, co-workers or parents.
- Stealing small items from employer, home or school.
- Secretive behavior regarding actions and possessions; poorly concealed attempts to avoid attention and suspicion such as frequent trips to storage rooms, restroom, basement, etc.

APPENDIX D   SIGNS OF STIMULANT ABUSE

Cocaine, crack, crank, speed, methamphetamimes

- Dilated pupils (when large amounts are taken).
- Dry mouth and nose, bad breath, frequent lip licking.
- Excessive activity, difficulty sitting still, lack of interest in food or sleep.
- Irritable, argumentative, nervous.
- Talkative, but conversations often lack continuity; changes subjects rapidly.
- Runny nose, cold or chronic sinus/nasal problems, nose bleeds.
- Use or possession of paraphernalia including small spoons, razor blades, mirror, little bottles of white powder and plastic, glass or metal straws.
- Small tin foil debris approximately 2 in square.
- Picking at skin to the point of creating sores.
- Habitually pulling out hair, often eyebrows, to the degree of baldness or complete absence of facial hair.

APPENDIX E   'MY NAME IS METH'

-

My Name Is Meth (Anon.)

I destroy homes. I tear families apart,
Take your children and that's just the start.
I'm more costly than diamonds, more precious than gold,
The sorrow I bring is a sight to behold.
If you need me, remember I'm easily found,
I live all around you – in schools and in town.
I live with the rich; I live with the poor,
I live down the street, and maybe next door.
I'm made in a lab, but not like you think,
I can be made under the kitchen sink.
In your child's closet, and even in the woods,
If this scares you to death, well it certainly should.
I have many names, but there's one you know best,
I'm sure you've heard of me, my name is crystal meth.
My power is awesome; try me you'll see,
But if you do, you may never break free.
Just try me once and I might let you go,

But try me twice, and I'll own your soul.
When I possess you, you'll steal and lie,
You do what you have to – just to get high.
The crimes you commit for my narcotics charms
Will be worth the pleasure you'll feel in my arms.
You'll lie to your mother; you'll lie to your dad,
When you see their tears, you should feel sad.
But you'll forget your morals and how you were raised,
I'll be your conscience, I'll teach you my ways.
I take kids from parents, and parents from kids,
I turn people from God, and separate friends.
I'll take everything from you, your books and your pride,
I'll be with you always, right by your side.
You'll give up everything – your family, your home,
Your friends, your money, and then you'll be alone.
I'll take and take, till you have nothing more to give,
When I'm finished with you, you'll be lucky to live.
If you try me be warned – this is no game,
If given a chance, I'll drive you insane.
I'll ravish your body; I'll control your mind,
I'll win you completely; your soul will be mine.
The nightmares I'll give you while lying in bed,
The voices you'll hear, from inside your head.
The sweats, the shakes, and the visions you'll see,
I want you to know, these are all gifts from me.
But then it's too late, and you'll know in your heart,
That you are mine, and we shall not part.
You'll regret that you tried me, they always do,
But you came to me, not I to you.
You knew this would happen, many times you were told,
But you challenged my power, and chose to be bold.
You could have said no, and just walked away,
If you could live that day over, now what would you say?
I'll be your master; you will be my slave,
I'll even go with you, when you go to your grave.
Now that you have met me, what will you do?
Will you try me or not? It's all up to you.
I can bring you more misery than word can tell,
Come take my hand, let me lead you to hell.

                    Unknown author: another Jane Doe

REFERENCES

BOOKS AND PUBLICATIONS

Amen, Dr Daniel G. (2002) *Making a Good Brain Great*. Berkley Trade.

Andreasen, Dr Nancy (2001) *Brave New Brain: Conquering Mental Illness in the Era of the Genome*. Oxford University Press, USA.

Dupont, Dr Robert (1977) *The Selfish Brain*, American Psychiatric Pub Group.

Fontaine, Claire and Fontaine, Mia (2006) *Comeback: A Mother and Daughter's Journey Through Hell and Back*. HarperCollins.

Grossman, Dave and DeGaetano, Gloria (1999) *Teaching our Kids to Kill: Call to Action Against TV, Movie and Video Game Violence*. Crown.

Harris, Judith Rich (1999) *The Nurture Assumption: Why Children Turn Out the Way They Do*. Free Press.

Holley, Dr Mary F. (2005) *Crystal Meth: They Call It Ice*. Tate Publishing.

Quartz, Steven R. and Sejnowski, Dr Terrence J. (2003) *Liars, Lovers, and Heroes: What the New Brain Science Reveals About How We Become Who We Are*. Harper.

Sommer, Carl (2004) *Character Under Attack and What You Can Do About It.* Advance Publishing.

INTERNET REFERENCES

Teens in Crisis http://teensncrisis.org/
Partnership for a Drug Free America http://www.drugfree.org/
Drug Enforcement Agency http://www.dea.gov/
Office of National Drug Control Policy http://www.whitehousedrugpolicy.gov/
Stop Drugs http://www.stopdrugs.org/methamphetamines.html
Parents Helping Teens http://tnc.parentshelpingteens.com/
Rape Drugs http://www.nyu.edu/odae/drdrugs.html
National Center for Missing and Abused Children http://www.missingkids.com/
Drug Testing http://www.psychemedics.com/
Methamphetamines http://www.intelligencesyboll.com/Methamphetamines.htm
Montana Meth Project: 'Not Even Once' http://notevenonce.com/